Becoming a Pioneer

— of —

SUCCESS

God's Plan to Help You
Win in Life and in Business

Becoming a Pioneer

~ of ~

SUCCESS

God's Plan to Help You
Win in Life and in Business

TRACEY
ARMSTRONG

ENDORSEMENTS

Tracey is bringing a much needed insight to all who have an other-focused desire to succeed. If you have ears to hear and eyes to see, then use them and launch into this book. The beginning of any great success story starts with the path being lit by an insight. I, for one, want to thank Tracey for putting a big lamp in our hand and sending us down our God-given path with confidence.

Coach Mike, Success Coach
Mindpill, Inc., Seattle, Washington

Tracey Armstrong is the embodiment of the incredible future we have in the Body of Christ. Tracey and his gifted wife, Nathalie, are anointed and articulate. They know truth, live truth, and express truth in a fresh way. Listen carefully, there is more than words on a page, more than words spoken—there is a voice within the voice. Hear it and be changed.

Tracey is a pioneer...nothing has come easy for him. Against all odds he came to his current status—one step, one challenge, one victory at a time. Tracey and Nathalie are not only impressive leaders for this generation, they are my friends. I'm proud to be in their world!

Pastor Phil Munsey
The Life Church, Mission Viejo, California

Tracey's passion to see people live life without limits is communicated clearly and effectively in his new book, *Becoming a Pioneer of Success*. As you journey through the pages, you will gain insight into the barriers that keep you from achieving, as well as develop tools for breaking through to the next level and beyond.

As someone who has personally benefited from Tracey's insight and coaching over the last 15 years, I encourage you to read this book, apply its truths, and fearlessly pursue your dreams.

Don Wiggins, Entrepreneur and Creator
Silverback Extreme Energy Drink, Corona, California

It is imperative that every leader and aspiring leader read *Becoming a Pioneer of Success*. In these pages, written by Tracey Armstrong, step-by-step coaching presents information about the skill and wisdom needed to move you beyond your own limited abilities. If followed, his practical advice will empower you to build a foundation for success in every area of your life, and alert you to the pitfalls that so often sidetrack those on the journey. I for one am anxious to put these truths into practice.

Michael McClellan, President
Colonial Foods, LLC
A 106 restaurant franchise of Pizza Hut

ACKNOWLEDGMENTS

I would like to thank my wife, Nathalie, for being my pioneering partner as we pave a new frontier and leap into new horizons for a new breed of pioneers who will follow. And thanks to our junior pioneers, our sons, Tristen and Yosef, who keep us searching for new and creative ways to leave a clear-cut road of success for them and their generation.

CONTENTS

THE SOUL OF A PIONEER

Beloved, I pray that you may prosper in all things and be in health, just as your soul prospers (3 John 1:2).

I have heard over the years that the soul is so complex that neither science nor religion can fully understand or comprehend it. I have also heard it said that the soul is the place in man where our thoughts, feelings, emotions, and intellect or mind reside; and I believe that this is true.

When I first committed my life to Christ, I was told to renew my mind (a main function of the soul). I was instructed to do so through reading the Word of God, and by studying and memorizing as much of it as I could, so it would help me overcome any obstacles and live life to the fullest. I sought for people who I could admire—who had more knowledge of the Word, had completed more study in the Word, and memorized more of the Word—but some of these people were still struggling with things that to me were unacceptable for a disciple of Christ.

Mixing Imagination With the Word of God

Personally, I discovered I could acquire more virtue and realize more change in my life from just one verse of the Bible once meditated on, than reading an entire chapter. Previously, while reading the Bible, I would see it as a story, but not directly applicable to me. Yet once I started meditating on the spiritual significance of each verse and carefully imagining myself living in that spiritual truth, my soul began to change. With each moment that my imagination interacted with the Word of God, pictures flashed through my mind, creating "possibility thoughts"—thoughts of overcoming temptation and improper addictions, thoughts of spiritual strength, and thoughts of prosperity.

The children of Israel were prohibited from entering the Promised Land because they hadn't mingled the Word of God with their imagination. It wasn't that they didn't believe that God could get them into the Promised Land, nor was it that they didn't believe that it was a real place. The Bible says they couldn't enter the land because they didn't mingle the Word of God with their imagination. They didn't envision themselves walking into the Promised Land; they didn't see themselves sitting around the fire eating the oversized grapes. Instead, they used their mental energies to compare their present situation with how things used to be, and to complain about the humble conditions of the journey. If they had spent more time meditating on the immense possibilities of their destination, they would have developed such a determination to get there, that their tongues would have tasted the milk and honey long before they actually experienced these pleasures! Even after Joshua and Caleb returned from the Promised Land with samples of the prosperity of the land and the children of Israel had actually tasted the fruit, they could still see themselves only as grasshoppers in the sight of their enemies—defeated, instead of prosperous.

THE STATE OF YOUR PROSPERITY
REFLECTS THE STATE OF YOUR SOUL

John writes in Third John 1:2 that God desires for us to prosper and be in health even as our soul prospers. This verse leaves a very clear picture in my mind that my soul, its health, and its prosperity is the pacesetter for all other aspects of my life and prosperity. Having an unhealthy soul, it is impossible to have faith; it is impossible to stay free; it is impossible to be prosperous. The state of your soul dictates the state of your health and lifestyle. The more positive you think, the more encouraged you feel, and the greater emotional health you possess. The more prosperous your soul, the more prosperous your life.

However, many people have worked hard in order to gain great success only to find they are still lacking something even after they have reached their goal in life. True prosperity is more than money or fame. True prosperity is having a healthy soul so that you can enjoy your earthly blessings and successes!

INSPIRED IMAGINATIONS

A healthy soul allows you to receive the images or pictures of possibilities that God shows each and every person—pictures of their possible future. These images are superimposed onto the imagination of man. Faith is impossible without using your imagination. Faith is something we all desire, yet faith is hard to maintain if your soul is unhealthy. Confidence, a synonym for faith, manifests in our soul—not within our spirit. However, we have given much more attention to becoming spiritual without the understanding that our soul must go through transformation in order to have all the benefits of spiritual grace. Just as James said that the tongue of man is like a rudder of a ship, steering and turning that person wherever it will lead them, so I believe that the imagination of man is the mast of that same ship, which receives the wind of inspiration that causes movement in man.

It was the wind of God that caused Christopher Columbus against all odds and myths to board a ship and sail across the Atlantic Ocean. Think of it—it wasn't the calculations of someone who had previously ventured out before him that gave him confidence; it was the inspiration of God that moved him to chart his course based on imaginary nautical lines. His inspiration came from vivid pictures etched into his mind by the revelatory thought that the world must be round even though popular opinion promoted the thought that the world was flat.

God is constantly blowing on the imagination of man. If you have ever said in your heart, *What if?* or *I wonder,* or *I think that might work,* then you may be receiving the same wind blowing upon your imagination that causes the world to flow in perfect balance on its axis. If you have ever heard someone say to you, "It has never been done that way before," or "That will never work," or even "Who do you think you are?" those words may be an indication that you have received an inspired thought from God in your imagination. There is a huge difference between a figment of your imagination and a God-inspired imagination. A figment is something that is not true and could never be true, yet a true imaginary thought is a God-inspired thought that will and can benefit you as well as others. Most figments are self-motivated, self-serving, and self-glorifying because they are self-induced or might even find their origin in the camp of the enemy. On the other hand, every true imaginary thought will benefit more than just the one who receives it.

MORE AND MORE NETHER-LANDS

Most people won't allow God to give them creative thoughts until they are confronted with an obstacle or need. For instance, before 1100 A.D., certain land of the Netherlands was suitable only for grazing sheep, due to the fact that during some seasons of the year, the land would flood or become extremely soggy. By 1100 A.D., the sea level started to rise and began to also flood the coastal villages. To correct the ocean's invasion, the people created dams to keep the water from encroaching upon their homes and businesses. Eventually they realized that if they could hold the water back, they could also regain lost land and even more land than they had before.

Because of the increase of the population of the Netherlands, the Dutch lords and royalty decided to build dikes off shore capturing the seawater and draining it back into the ocean leaving new dry land. As they drained the water, they uncovered rich, fertile land. Even to this day, the Dutch from time to time will add more land by building dikes and draining the seawater. The Dutch are now experts at conquering the ocean. Some residents can easily find seashells in their backyards. Often old war artifacts such as mines, sunken warships, and shot-down war planes are uncovered.

Today more than half of the Netherlands is below sea level. Just imagine what Holland would look like if the Dutch had never believed in or searched for a solution. The Dutch show us that you are conquered only when you stop fighting. If you never quit, your creative imagination will make a way for victory. This is a wonderful gift from God.

GILLETTE'S BRILLIANT IDEA

When King Camp Gillette's home burned in the Chicago Fire of 1871, he was forced to become a traveling salesman in order to support his family. While working, he met a man by the name of William Painter, the inventor of the disposable Crown Cork bottle cap, who told Gillette that a successful invention was one that was purchased over and over by satisfied customers.

Years passed while Gillette tried to discover that truly genuine idea, but without success. Then suddenly in 1895 while shaving, Gillette had a brilliant idea. A razor with a safe, inexpensive, and disposable blade *flashed into his mind.*

This was the beginning of the disposable movement, which we presently enjoy. Now we not only have disposable razors, but also disposable cameras, disposable napkins, and we can't forget disposable diapers. (Thank God for disposable diapers. Have you ever dunked a diaper into a toilet?)

Let me ask you a question! How many times has some great and brilliant idea passed through your mind without you doing anything about bringing it to life? If you say, "Many times," then this book is for you.

It took six years for the Gillette razor to evolve. Technical expert after expert tried to discourage Gillette, telling him it would be impossible to develop steel that was hard, thin, and inexpensive enough in order to commercialize the disposable razor blade. Finally, he found one man who was willing to try and who succeeded in 1903—William Nickerson.

King Camp Gillette was someone who did not know the meaning of the word *quit*. He became the inventor of the first disposable razor then known as the "Safety Razor," which was patented on November 15, 1904.

Off and running, the Gillette Safety Razor Company began operation in south Boston, and sales continued to grow steadily. The U.S. Government issued Gillette safety razors to its entire armed forces during World War I because recent studies in that day showed that shaving was hygienic for the soldiers in the field. Some 3.5 million razors and 32 million blades were put into military hands, and in doing so, the entire nation was converted to the Gillette safety razor.

RELEASE THE PIONEER!

That last flash, that last idea you allowed to blow past you last year or even ten years ago may very well be the next truly original idea that the world has been waiting for. Continue to journey with me through these pages and unleash the pioneer inside of you. Genius is available to you. The keys to pioneering are within your grasp, yes even in your hands right now. Read on and become one of God's *new-day pioneers of success.*

CHAPTER ONE

THE DESTINED YOU

But indeed for this purpose I have raised you up, that I may show My power in you, and that My name may be declared in all the earth (Exodus 9:16).

MISUNDERSTOOD DREAMS

"Brothers, listen to my dream," exclaimed Joseph as he ran out of his tent. "We all were working in the field gathering sheaves, when my sheaf grew and became greater than yours. Suddenly, your sheaves gathered around mine and bowed down to mine." Appalled at the audacity of what the dream suggested, Joseph's brothers verbally scolded him for being excited about such a thought. "Do you intend to reign over us?" they indignantly asked.

A few days later, Joseph bounded from his tent in the early morning and excitedly proclaimed, "I had yet another dream— I want to tell you this one as well." His brothers protested, "We don't want to hear anymore from this arrogant dreamer." Their father, Jacob, quickly silenced the whole family and motioned Joseph to continue. Judah rolled his eyes with disgust. "This one was even greater than the one before," said Joseph. "The sun, the moon, and eleven stars bowed down to me." Jacob, taken by surprise, rebuked him, saying, "So, what now? Do you expect your mother and me, along with your brothers, to worship you?"

Joseph's dreams, or creative thoughts sent from God, triggered envy in his brothers but caused his father to ponder over the matter. People who experience creative thoughts, such as Joseph had, will always experience reproach or misunderstanding. We see this throughout many examples in the Bible. Noah was mocked because there had never been rain, and yet he was building a boat on dry land. Pharaoh and his magicians ridiculed Moses when he envisioned liberty for the children of Israel and asked for the slaves to be set free. Jesus was ridiculed by the multitudes when He declared that He was the bread of life from Heaven, and the list goes on. Once you pursue destiny instead of default, you will hear, "It has never been done that way," or "That will never work," or even, "Who do you think you are?"

Created for a Special Purpose

People who live by creative thoughts live according to a mandate that must be fulfilled before they can finish their destiny; anything less is simply default and is not worth living for. We have been promised that "...it shall come to pass in the last days, says God, that I will pour out of My Spirit on all flesh; your sons and your daughters shall prophesy, your young men shall see visions, your old men shall dream dreams" (Acts 2:17). Without creative thoughts we would suffer from a lack of mental focus or faith. Mental focus keeps us on track; it allows us to stand even when we are thrown into a dark pit and sold to our enemy by the ones whom we love, as was in the case of Joseph.

Joseph needed to learn how to go after his destiny even when his family didn't agree with it and ridiculed him. To move as Joseph did—from the pit, to the governor's house, to the prison, to the palace where he maintained authority, then finally serving without malice those who once rejected him—could not have been accomplished without a sense of destiny. Likewise, you need a sense of destiny to allow you to grow and mature in grace and mercy, simply because life itself and satan will challenge your destiny.

Every human being should have a sense of purpose, a sense that he was created for something special. *Special* doesn't necessarily have to be grand or historical. It simply means that God has placed a divine sense of purpose inside each person. Solomon said in the Book of Ecclesiastes, "He has made everything beautiful in its time. He also has planted eternity in men's hearts and minds [a divinely implanted sense of a purpose working through the ages which nothing under the sun but God alone can satisfy], yet so that man cannot find out what God has done from the beginning to the end" (Eccl. 3:11 AMP).

ON THE SAME PAGE WITH GOD

There is a God-inspired blueprint that has been predestined for you. However, it is up to you to line up with the predetermined will and desire of God, and collaborate with the purposes of God in order to accomplish God's dream, even while life and the enemies of destiny try to choke out this sense of purpose as well as the creativity to accomplish the task.

God is the Creator of mankind and the Father of those who have received His Son, Jesus. And like any other father, His desire is that we are successful according to the divine blueprint that He has drawn for our lives. Nonetheless, it is up to you and me to search our own hearts and to find the source of passion that will motivate and move us into our destiny.

In the following pages, you will learn how to search the heart of God for detailed instruction on how to build your life according to this divinely implanted sense of purpose. You will see the blueprint for your life and discover the missing link that solves the "riddle of life." If you follow the instructions in these chapters, you will find the secrets that many great men and women have understood—the power of success, the power of invention, the power of greatness. You will learn to live according to the power of creative thought, which comes only from God.

Success is our God-given right. Before the serpent came to deceive our forefathers, there was nothing but success, because that is God's will for us. We all want success; it comes when plain desire is transformed into calculated planned action. I believe that when you realize the *desire* of your heart, it is confirmation that God has given you the jurisdiction to pursue that which you long and hope for. I am not speaking about lust, but *desire*—there is a difference. God becomes the author of the desires of your heart. He transplants His purpose, will, and commitment into you. And God is more than willing to give us the gifts, talent, or the power it takes to accomplish our heart's desire if we share our passions with Him.

Creative thought comes from being willing to trust in the fact that this feeling of purpose and conviction of success is more than a good idea that just happened to leap into your heart one day. You must be fully persuaded and possess a sense of destiny. Once this sense of destiny is instilled in you, God will deliver to you the desire to accomplish His predetermined blueprint for your life. In actuality, God gives you the desire that you feel every day, as well as the help you need to accomplish the desire.

For it is God who works in you both to will and to do for His good pleasure (Philippians 2:13).

The best life to live is the one that your Creator has purposed for you to live. God created each and every one of us with something specific and wonderful in mind. The "pot" doesn't say to the Potter, "I don't want to be a pot; I want to be a statue." Otherwise, the pot would be worthless to the Potter when the Potter needed something to pour water from. But if the pot would rejoice in its purpose and fulfill its purpose well, then the Potter would use the pot often. If you are experiencing a sense of dissatisfaction of purpose in your heart, it may be that God is working with you so that *His* desires become *your* heart's desire, and you will accomplish what you have been designed to accomplish. Once you can clearly see the blueprint of your life, then and only then will you be able to accomplish that design.

SEEING WITH SPIRITUAL EYES

The Bible is a great source of success principles for everyone. However, we must also learn to receive revelation from God regarding His individual plan and desire for each of our lives. Neither the natural eye nor the natural ear will be able to know the plans that God has for us. Only the Spirit of God can show us what God has prepared for us individually, and He will search the heart of man in order to reveal, remove, and replace anything contrary to the blueprint, allowing us to compare spiritual things with spiritual things (see 1 Cor. 2:13).

Even though you will fulfill your destiny in the natural, you must first receive insight through spiritual methods. You must be able to know the thoughts, desires, and intentions of God. The Bible calls this "the mind of Christ" (see 1 Cor. 2:9-16). As long as you rely on what you see in the natural, you will be limited to dwell and act according to the indications of your natural surroundings and circumstances. Yet if I can teach you to step into the ability to see spiritually, you will intertwine your spirit with the Spirit of God, which will create limitless power. Your spiritual eyes are the key to your future and purpose.

Jesus went away and sent the Spirit of Truth to guide you and lead you into everything that has been prepared for you. The Spirit of God is always hearing instruction from the Father to lead you into the next step of your destiny. The Spirit of God is committed to help you and has been given authority to guide you into your destiny. The Bible calls Him our Helper, our Teacher, and our Comforter. God's goal is that the Spirit of Truth would lead you so that He can show you the possible future (see Jn. 16:13-16). The images of your future can never be understood by might or by power; but by the Spirit of God, we must see into the future. We must see the way to overcome the obstacles.

SEEING LAUNCHES DESIRING

People often ask me how I can see things in the spirit when they cannot see past their natural circumstances and obstacles. I have discovered that sight and desire are closely connected. Without a fiery desire, you will not have the conviction to believe in your purpose, and in order to fan the right desires, you must understand what you see.

An angel appeared and spoke to Zerubbabel, "What do you see?" Zerubbabel described what he saw. Zerubbabel saw clearly, yet when the angel asked, "Do you understand what you see?" Zerubbabel replied, "No, my Lord." The angel replied, "Not by might nor by power, but by My Spirit." It's by the Spirit of God that we can understand the mysteries of life (see Zech. 4:6).

Once you see your destiny clearly, the sight of it will create the desire to achieve it. Desire must overwhelm you, in order for you to achieve what you see. Desire will give you the determination to overcome any obstacles that would try to hold you from your goal. Desire will replace vague hope with passion. In order for you to achieve greatness, you must become emotionally involved with the vision. This can be accomplished only by seeing yourself in the finished work. When you can see yourself having accomplished what you dreamed, at that moment the zeal of passion will overwhelm you with a great desire, giving you the strength and fortitude to leap over any obstacles and break free from all limitations.

God finished everything that He planned, the day that He spoke it. He spoke our destiny before He established the foundations of the earth and called it finished. What God has intended for you has already been predetermined. So when you determine to pursue what you see, only then will your determination link with God's predetermination, and He will impart a supernatural force to help you live in what God has already finished.

> *For we who have believed do enter that rest, as He has said: "So I swore in My wrath, 'They shall not enter My rest,'" although the works were finished from the foundation of the world* (Hebrews 4:3).

GOD-GIVEN CREATIVITY

So God truly gives you the desires of your heart. Once you gain a desire, then you will receive the creativity to accomplish the desire. It is God who establishes in you both the determination and creativity for His pleasure, which is to finish His perfected purpose through you. Mankind has often thought that God would do everything for him. Yet the ability and liberty to do what we can see has been given to us by God. This is His divine order; He planned it this way. We must understand that God has placed within us the power to create what we see. Desire enables you to tap into His creative power; that creative power is the imagination of God.

Countless times, I have seen it work like this: Desire will create passion, and passion will then override fear and limitation. Sometimes you will clearly see how things should be, but realize you are not living in what you see, which will cause dissatisfaction in your soul. Dissatisfaction will then create a determination inside of you to change what is seen in the natural into what is known and seen in the spirit realm.

Dissatisfaction can be a positive emotion when mingled with God's creative imagination. While creative thought shows you what is possible, dissatisfaction can also cause you to dream of what could be. Dissatisfaction exists when your desire does not match your circumstances. Dissatisfaction in itself is destructive when left to run its course; it must be replaced with creative thought before it reaches despair and hopelessness. Creative thought gives you a new outlook on the circumstances that first caused you to be dissatisfied. When dissatisfaction triggers creative thought, it creates the motivation to accomplish your desire.

Indifference is the curse of laziness and hopelessness. A person without passion for God, His Kingdom, or His purpose for his life, is an ungodly person. God's creation should have a desire to fulfill the utmost potential of success, whether it's through instinct as in the animal kingdom or by moral obligation as with mankind. Mankind has an obligation to God to dream and think big. We were created in the image of God; we possess the power to dream and carry out our dreams just as our Father has.

Remember, tapping into God's creative imagination is *the* key to accomplishing success. Jesus Himself said that He could do nothing in His own power, but everything He did was accomplished by His ability to see in the Spirit and to hear in the Spirit. For what He saw and heard in the Spirit was from His Father. He saw what His Father wanted to complete and followed the Father's determination. We must follow the will of God in order to have great success. Once you see what is possible through creative thought, you will never be satisfied until you are walking in what you see. You will become so emotionally driven that you will do whatever needs to be done and change whatever needs to be changed to have what you see. It is not too hard to let go of sin when it is clearly marked as a hindrance to the destiny you are passionately pursuing.

God will use the emotion of desire to purge you from character flaws and dysfunctions. If you tell a person that he needs to stop being a certain way without giving him a reason to change, he will most likely refuse or fail to change. Yet if you tell someone that he can achieve the goal that he greatly desires by simply making a few changes, then he will be willing to change for the sake of the end result. The obstacle and pressure will disappear in the view of a new focal point. Creative thought gives you a new focal point causing you to focus on what is possible rather than focusing on what you will have to lay aside or overcome.

When my wife, Nathalie, was in labor giving birth to our sons, as her labor coach I had to encourage her to focus on breathing intensely and deeply. The goal was to achieve a completely relaxed and limp body during each contraction so that the labor would progress quickly and effectively. Focusing on breathing and relaxing from head to toe helped her endure the labor without being overwhelmingly focused on the pain. Likewise, the Spirit of God is our labor coach, encouraging us to focus on a future goal. He is distracting us from the temporary pain of change and the limitations of life while He births creative thoughts in our heart.

There should be a picture in your mind, a desire in your heart, and a creative thought from God that knits the previous two together propelling you into your destiny.

— CHAPTER TWO —

YOUR SUCCESS COACH

*But the anointing which you have received from Him abides
in you, and you do not need that anyone teach you; but as the
same anointing teaches you concerning all things, and is
true, and is not a lie, and just as it has taught you, you will
abide in Him* (1 John 2:27).

THE COACH

Mentors, think tanks, mastermind networks, success coach-
es...these terms are increasingly popular in the business world
nowadays. People are finding out they cannot accomplish success on their own. Why should they, if they can learn all the ins
and outs of success from someone who has already accomplished
what they are ambitiously pursuing? Why invent the wheel when
someone else has already successfully done so? Let's think about
it. Successful people already know the work ethic, responsibility,
and determination it takes to accomplish what you desire, and
they most likely have already sorted out potential problems,

which you can avoid. A mentor or success coach is a definite asset to anyone who has a heart to succeed.

I personally act as a success coach for a few businessmen and women. They call me when they need prayer, advice, or godly instruction. They call me when a big deal is on the table. I am not your normal success coach, though, imparting my own wisdom; instead, I go to my personal Success Coach and receive relevant wisdom for them from Him. People often express amazement at the wisdom that comes from my Success Coach, and I tell them that following His orders guarantees sure success.

Many years ago, I found the two most powerful sources of success—the Word of God and the Spirit of God. These two sources have become the foundation of any success coaching that I provide for the people in my life and for the success I have experienced so far.

In this chapter, I want to introduce you to my Success Coach, and in a later chapter, I will reveal to you the influence of the Bible as a success resource or manual. My Success Coach is all-knowing, omnipresent, and all-powerful; He is the Holy Spirit.

EQUIPPED FOR GREATNESS

In the 14th chapter of the Book of John, there are some dynamic revelations about our privileges in God—how He helps us, teaches us, and creates a place of success for us. Verse 12 says that we as believers will be able to do greater works than Jesus has done. I have always understood that to mean that we will perform greater miracles than Jesus was able to perform on the earth—not because Jesus was limited in any way, but because any good father or mentor desires for his pupil to surpass him. When we do these greater works, it confirms the greatness of our Teacher.

Even though "greater" can involve miracles, it also includes greater success. The word "greater" that Jesus used means to have a greater degree of whatever He was having—to have a larger portion. Now, it would be foolish for someone to think that Jesus was not successful or to think He did not accomplish what He came to earth to do. Jesus was certainly successful in His calling, and He completely accomplished what He was sent to do. And even more so, with Jesus as our teacher, mentor, and trainer, we should ultimately experience success, when we are good and obedient disciples.

Eventually, the Holy Spirit was sent to continue the coaching that Jesus started with His disciples. He was sent to make sure that we continued in the pattern of Jesus' limitless success. But before Jesus told us about the Holy Spirit, He told us about how to walk in the greater things of God.

TO LOVE IS TO OBEY AND TO OBEY IS TO SUCCEED

Jesus said, "If you love Me, keep My commandments" (Jn. 14:15). Godly success is based upon love. Godly love is absolutely unselfish. Godly love is morally and socially just. What does that mean? Being *morally just* means that you would never do anything to hurt the one that you love, and being *socially just* means that you desire to be with that person more than you desire to be with anyone else. Love is the doorway to God. Love opens our heart to hear from God and to obey what He speaks. God is love.

Verse 15 has confused me because I previously assumed that when Jesus said, "Keep My commandments," He was talking about the Ten Commandments or the Torah. Meanwhile, as a Christian, I was taught that the laws and statutes of God were fulfilled in Christ and that we needed to live according to the law of the Spirit of life in Christ Jesus. I understood that when I love my wife and children, this law of love demands far more from me than simply keeping the Ten Commandments. I do not need to remind myself to not kill them or steal from them, because my love for them would not even consider such despicable behavior.

So with this teaching in my heart, it was hard for me to understand what Jesus meant by "keep My commandments." I felt these words were a contradiction of everything that I had learned. However, after many years and a little research, I finally realized what Jesus was saying. I researched the word "commandment," which is the Greek word *entole* (en-tol-ay'), which means, "to receive and live in God's injunction or authoritative prescription." In this verse, "commandment" is not binding us to a legal system of control; it is releasing us to hear and receive authoritative instructions from God that will lead us in life—prescriptions that order our steps and lead us into greener pastures.

Our great physician Jesus interacts with us when we have moral and social love in our hearts for Him. He gives us a checkup by taking our spiritual, emotional, and mental temperature. After He diagnoses the problems or sicknesses in our life, He gives us a prescription that only the Author of life and wholeness could give—an authoritative prescription. Who knows better how to live your life than the One who created you and designed you for life? Your Coach can give you the solution for any problem, mess, or mistake if you can love Him enough to seek Him. You must spend time with Him and listen to what He has to say about anything and anybody. This doesn't mean that God restricts His authoritative prescription to only those who love Him; it does mean that if *you* don't love Him, *you* will never hear and obey Him.

It's not enough to just receive an authoritative prescription; you must also have the fortitude to obey the authoritative prescription in order to receive the miracle-working power of the prescription. Anyone can go to the doctor and receive a prescription, but the prescription works only when we take the medicine. Without a doubt, God's prescription will always bring health and wholeness. We can get a prescription for any circumstance in life;

we just have to be willing to hear, receive, and do what is instructed by God.

This Scripture reveals that when we love God, we will be able to receive life-changing instruction from Him. We must learn to be led by the Spirit. Romans 8:14 says, "For as many as are led by the Spirit of God, these are sons of God." God is not just looking for someone to carry out mighty works on earth; He is looking for people who will seek Him, give themselves over to Him, obey His prescriptions, and thus become heirs in His Kingdom. How do we do that? Simply by hearing and obeying the things God asks of us.

HOLY SPIRIT, A HELPER AT ALL TIMES AND A TEACHER OF ALL THINGS

Jesus made it very clear that He was going away, and in His place, He would send the Holy Spirit to help us (see Jn. 14:16). The Holy Spirit would come as our intercessor, our counselor, and our advocate who would coexist with us. He does so many wonderful things, and once you receive Him and experience His help, you will wonder why you were ever trying to do anything without Him. The Holy Spirit is here on earth to abide with us, to teach us, to lead us, to console us, to tell us what the Father says, to manifest Jesus in us, and to help us accomplish our assignments on earth. What a wealth of resource we have in Him!

There is a myth believed by some Christians that says the Holy Spirit and His gifts are good only for spiritual things. This myth has caused people to think that they do not need the gifts of the Holy Spirit to be successful in natural things, and may even find it necessary to separate themselves from the unction of the Spirit of God. Many believers think that any manifestation of the Holy Spirit is inappropriate in a secular or business setting, and should be confined to a church or Bible study setting. The common understanding especially in the charismatic world is that the Holy Spirit makes you goofy, extravagant, and spiritually eccentric. This is not true! A man's soul may react strangely when he encounters the Holy Spirit, but a person operating in the gifts of the Spirit does not need to act bizarre. People become strange because they have an unhealthy soul—a soul that doesn't know how to process what God is doing and doesn't understand what His intentions are for the world. Whereas, the Holy Spirit makes you wise, prudent, able, systematic, and fruitful.

Some businesspeople think that they have to stay "grounded" to natural things in order to be great businessmen and women. However, they misunderstand that God is the best businessman who ever lived. I think the real issue is whether or not you want God to rule and reign in your life, and that includes your business. You receive His rule and reign by acknowledging and receiving His corporate Advisor who He has sent to oversee the work on earth. John 14:26 says, "But the Helper, the Holy Spirit, whom the Father will send in My name, He will teach you all things, and bring to your remembrance all things that I said to you." The Holy Spirit is first your teacher. He can teach you about business. He can teach you about parenting. He can teach you about life in general. There is absolutely no area of life that the Holy Spirit cannot instruct you in. This passage clearly states, "He will teach you all things."

Another verse in the Bible says, "But the anointing which you have received from Him abides in you, and you do not need that anyone teach you; but as the same anointing teaches you concerning all things, and is true, and is not a lie, and just as it has taught you, you will abide in Him" (1 Jn. 2:27). The Bible uses the word "teacher" to describe the Holy Spirit, but for the sake of clarification, I will use the term "coach." This word gives the idea that He will not only instruct you, but that He will walk you through; and that when you forget who you are, He will remind you. The Holy Spirit will also bring to your remembrance what Christ has said to you and about you.

In a world full of deception, we need all the help we can get when it comes to discerning what is right and what is wrong. The Holy Spirit will not only help us clearly hear what God is saying, but He will also help us discern what the devil is doing. We have a promise in John 16:13 that the Holy Spirit will be the Spirit of truth to us. As the Spirit of truth, "He will guide you into all truth." We have a guide, someone who knows the way, someone who has experience and is able to get us through anything that life will send our way. He is such a good guide that He can hear from Heaven and tell you what is coming your way.

> However, when He, the Spirit of truth, has come, He will guide you into all truth; for He will not speak on His own authority, but whatever He hears He will speak; and He will tell you things to come (John 16:13).

The last thing I want to point out is that in this passage, the Spirit of truth will hear from Heaven and tell us what Heaven has to say about our past, present, and future. We can know the future—we must know the future—and the Holy Spirit will warn us of any pitfalls that will hinder our success as well as show us what will lead us into success.

God does not want us to be ignorant. He doesn't want us to live in the dark but wants us to clearly understand everything that is happening in our lives.

When Weakness Is Strength

A good coach will help you recognize your weaknesses and show you how to overcome them, making them your strengths. This is exactly what your Coach, the Holy Spirit, does. He goes beyond showing you your weaknesses; He helps you overcome them and totally separates you from your weakness as He intercedes on your behalf. He makes your weak place a strong place.

As Christians, strength is not found in our abilities. Our strength lies in our vulnerability to Christ and willingness to be led by the Spirit of God. The Bible is very clear about this. If we could obtain everlasting life through our own efforts, Jesus would have never needed to die on the cross. If we could live life without a Comforter and Helper, then Jesus would have never prayed for the Holy Spirit to be sent to replace Him on earth. But Jesus knew that life would be impossible for us without help. Because our natural instinct is to fulfill our appetites, He prayed that God would send the Spirit of Holiness to live with us and be in us. Since the fall of man, the nature of mankind has been weak, and we need to realize that we can be strong only through the help of the Holy Spirit.

Even in our greatest genius and in our greatest strength, we are unable to stand in the place of God. First Corinthians 1:25 says, "Because the foolishness of God is wiser than men, and the weakness of God is stronger than men." We should become fools in our own sight by allowing God to make us wise, and we should become weak in our own eyes by allowing Him to make us strong. I would rather be an idiot in Christ than to be a know-it-all in the world. The Holy Spirit truly enjoys teaching, training, and coaching. If we give Him the opportunity, He will teach us anything and everything we need to know. However, we must reconcile to the reality that we alone don't know everything. Paul the apostle, one of the greatest men of God who has ever lived, wrote that God's strength can function only when it has a place of weakness to operate in.

> And He said to me, "My grace is sufficient for you, for My strength is made perfect in weakness." Therefore most gladly I will rather boast in my infirmities, that the power of Christ may rest upon me. Therefore I take pleasure in infirmities, in reproaches, in needs, in persecutions, in distresses, for Christ's sake. For when I am weak, then I am strong (2 Corinthians 12:9-10).

Paul would rather have been vulnerable to God by admitting his weakness than to have all the strength of the world, because

Paul understood that God's strength is supernatural and not limited to the natural. If a person arrogantly thinks he knows the way to his destination, he will not be able to change his mind until he has figured out that he has no idea of where he is going. But once he sees clearly that he is lost, he should be willing to ask for directions. And God waits until we are ready to ask Him for guidance and directions.

PRAYER IS THE KEY

Often, when a person is at the end of his rope and has nowhere else to turn, he looks up. Consequently, when someone looks up, God comes down and rescues him. A Christian who doesn't live in the Spirit is like a fish out of water, constantly trying to flop back into the water when it lacks oxygen. But in order to thrive, rather than simply trying to cope with one emergency after another, it is very important that we learn to live in the Spirit and learn to be led by the Spirit. Living in the Spirit of God is the only way to tap into the super-nature of God, where no weakness dwells.

> *Likewise the Spirit also helps in our weaknesses. For we do not know what we should pray for as we ought, but the Spirit Himself makes intercession for us with groanings which cannot be uttered* (Romans 8:26).

The Holy Spirit is not just assigned, but *co-assigned* to you, because His purpose concerning you is to *coexist* with you. His assignment is to help you in your infirmities and weaknesses and to lead you through anything that could hinder your development and success. The original Greek word used for "weaknesses" in this passage describes anything that may be lacking in spirit, soul, and body. This leaves you without excuse for perpetually living with any weaknesses that you may have.

Here you see the key to living in the supernatural—prayer!...yet not just a simple prayer, because you don't know how to pray properly. Rather, you should be led by the Spirit and full of the Spirit in your prayer. In charismatic circles, we understand this to mean to pray in our heavenly language. As we pray in tongues, we allow the Holy Spirit to pray for us and on our behalf. As we exercise this gift, the Holy Spirit will begin to reveal our weaknesses to us. His goal in showing us our weakness is not to stop us or slow us down, but He desires to show us where we need His help. Once we realize that we need His help, we will then allow Him to intercede on our behalf. The most common understanding of intercession is to pray on the behalf of someone else. This definition is true, yet it is not the full meaning of intercession.

Remember, the Holy Spirit's desire is to make you strong where you are weak and His assignment is to help us. The word used for "help" in verse 26 means "to be joined, to stand on the behalf of," or again, "to be co-assigned."

After you are convicted of your weaknesses, the Holy Spirit will relieve you of your burden and will stand in that place of weakness for you, making it strong. He wants to fill that place instead of you filling that place with your inabilities. I play on our church softball team and some of my teammates have knee problems. This makes it hard for them to run all the bases. After they hit the ball and run to first base, they have the option of receiving help, an intercessor, or as we say in the softball league, a relief runner. If they choose to receive help, they can go back to the bench and watch someone run for them. Although they are not participating as a runner (the place of their weakness,) they still remain a part of the game. This is exactly what the Holy Spirit does for us. We have the choice to call for relief, and He will come, setting us free from our weaknesses without taking us out of the game. You don't have to live in your weakness and suffer its effects. You don't have to live with your past failures. You don't have to live in pain. But through prayer, you can allow the Holy Spirit to be your relief and make your life much easier and lighter. Wherever you are weak, He can be strong on your behalf if you allow Him to be.

It gets even better—He doesn't stop at this point of inter-cession of praying for you and standing in your weak places. He continues by searching your heart to make sure you have the true view of who you are in Christ and where you are going on your journey.

He Will Free Your Mind and Restore Your Soul

I had always been taught that the Christian life is only about our spirituality. I now know that we cannot be strong spiritual people if we have weak souls. Our soul is made up our thoughts, feelings, and emotions. When I received my call to the ministry, I asked God what I was to take to His Church. He simply said, "Take them My thoughts, feelings, and intentions." The King-dom of God that is within you is limited to residing in you if you are struggling with fear, jealousy, pride, shame, guilt, self-pity, blame, timidity, perversion, selfishness, etc. We can have almighty God living inside us; but if we don't take care of our soul to make it healthy, then the Kingdom of God within us is limited in its expression according to what our soul will allow.

I believe that the Holy Spirit has come to help us renew our mind and help us regenerate our soul. Take a moment to think about it. Think about all the traits of the Holy Spirit. What is He up to? He teaches us, convicts us, searches our minds, restores our soul, give us gifts that increase by the reason of use, leads us, and shows us the path of righteousness because He is the Spirit of holiness. And of course, He does even much more than that. If we still think with limitation when God has given us unlimit-ed favor and abilities, we will continue to live in limitation be-cause our soul has not changed. Consider the example of the slaves who were set free in American history. Many of them chose not to leave their slave masters because they had never ex-perienced freedom and knew nothing different from bondage.

Those who were born free, however, and who had been cap-tured and brought to America, longed for that freedom.

When people come to Christ as slaves, we may declare them to be free from the slave master but that is not enough. We need to send them through rehabilitation, helping them deal with their thoughts, feelings, and emotions. We need to help them process life differently; we need to teach them that they don't have the same limits they once knew. Probably the most impor-tant thing would be to give them a reason to be free and stay free. People sabotage their success by continuing to practice old patterns or by relapsing into the old habits of their soul. The Holy Spirit wants to help us by showing us the future—a future that is ordained by God.

> *Now He who searches the hearts knows what the mind of the Spirit is, because He makes intercession for the saints accord-ing to the will of God* (Romans 8:27).

The Holy Spirit searches the *kardia* (kar-dee´-ah), which means "the heart (figuratively), the thoughts, or feelings (mind)." The Holy Spirit investigates our thoughts and feelings, taking inventory of our perspectives on what God has deter-mined for our life. He knows and sees everything that is in our heart—not just the things we are willing to acknowledge, but also the things we are hiding. Eventually, the secret places of the heart must be confronted because they hinder who you are to become.

Initially, the Holy Spirit reveals to us our weaknesses so that we will invite Him to help us. He then begins to talk to God the Father as if it were He Himself who needed help. Once He has freedom to make that area strong, as our helper He shares in our infirmities and replaces them with His strength. God doesn't want us to always be weak; He wants to fill that place of weakness until He can renew our mind to what God's will for our life is. God's will for your life is not defeat, but victory; it is not failure, but success. Godly success requires that you live in the Spirit and are led by the Spirit.

FAILURES AND FAMILIES ARE NO EXCUSE

Once again, the children of Israel were seeking deliverance from their enemies—this time from the Midianites. The Midianites had moved into Israel territory and forcefully made it their own. Their herds ate much of the grass, destroying Israel's resources and causing great grief. Over time, poverty came upon the children of Israel, and so they prayed and asked God to help them. God chose to raise up a young man by the name of Gideon.

When the angel of the Lord came to encourage Gideon to live in the anointing that God had given Him, he found Gideon threshing wheat in a wine press, although the wine press should have been used for making wine. Yet because of his fear of the Midianites, Gideon used the wine press for a hiding place while he worked. These were poor working conditions, to say the least. Actually, in order to properly thresh wheat, you need to be able to separate the chaff of the wheat from the fruit of the wheat. In the days of Gideon, this process was usually done on a rocky cliff where there was ample wind to remove the chaff, which is the lightweight husk around the fruit of the wheat.

To make matters worse, while Gideon was attempting to thresh wheat in a most inappropriate place, the wine makers were unable to produce wine because Gideon was occupying the wine press. These circumstances limited the Israelites to what they could produce, causing more poverty and frustration.

In Judges chapter 6, when the angel appeared to Gideon, he said, "The Lord is with you, you mighty man of valor!" (Judg. 6:12b) In the New Testament, we gain a greater understanding of this anointing. When the anointing of God rests upon you, the Lord is with you (see Acts 10:38). The anointing of the Holy Spirit enabled people to do supernatural things in the Old

Testament just as it does today. Gideon, however, immediately had objections to becoming the deliverer of Israel. He excused himself because of past disappointments and frustrations. He said, "O my lord, if the Lord is with us, why then has all this happened to us? And where are all His miracles which our fathers told us about, saying, 'Did not the Lord bring us up from Egypt?' But now the Lord has forsaken us and delivered us into the hands of the Midianites" (Judg. 6:13). Gideon obviously had some strongholds He was dealing with.

But the angel of the Lord would not be stopped by these objections. The angel of the Lord knew that Gideon had favor from God and that God was with him, so his past failures and past disappointments didn't matter. The angel was trying to renew his mind to the possibilities of the future. In verse 14, the original text does not use the term "the angel of the Lord," but says, "the Lord," meaning Jehovah looked upon him and said, "Go in this might of yours...Have I not sent you?" Here we see God Himself working on Gideon's mind-set. If Gideon had continued to not believe in himself or in the fact that God had ordained and sent him, then the anointing on his life would have been in vain. But God never does anything in vain; instead, He continues working on a person until that person believes what God has said about him.

Gideon still wasn't convinced though. When He realized that God wasn't going to let him off the hook because of his past, He tried using his family as an excuse. I love God's response to this excuse. He says, "Surely I will be with you, and you shall defeat the Midianites as one man" (Judg. 6:16). God was saying to Gideon, "Don't worry, I will be fighting with you. Don't worry about your heritage; you can leave your family at home. You will overcome all the Midianites as an individual."

DESTINED TO WIN

Although Gideon continued to need convincing, God never gave up. He continued working on Gideon all the way up until the day that Gideon defeated the Midianites and their allies. We see it in Judges 7:25: "And they captured two princes of the Midianites, Oreb and Zeeb. They killed Oreb at the rock of Oreb, and Zeeb they killed at the winepress of Zeeb. They pursued Midian and brought the heads of Oreb and Zeeb to Gideon on the other side of the Jordan."

First they captured the tyrants, and then they took Oreb whose name means, "raven." Ravens are aggressive birds, and when they attack, they go for the eyes, trying to impair the vision of its victim. The devil knows that if he can steal your vision, he can steal your joy, your favor, your provision, and your future. Gideon took his raven to the rock, the rock of Oreb, which was a rocky cliff. There are two things here that you must recognize: First, Gideon pursued his enemy to the rock. The Rock is the only place we can receive restored vision; the Rock is the only place we can again receive our sight. Jesus is our Rock! Secondly, Gideon cut off his enemy's head at the place where he should have been threshing wheat. Gideon refused to be intimidated anymore. He was not going to allow his past to destroy his future; his days of hiding were over. He refused to accept defeat and was making strides toward success. His mind or soul was renewed to what God purposed for him, and He refused to live in anything less than the best that God had for him. He had a transformation in his soul.

But Gideon was not finished. He then took Zeeb, another prince of Midian, to the winepress. Zeeb means "wolf," again an aggressive animal. A wolf preys on weakness and vulnerability. A lack of vision makes you weak; a lack of foresight makes you vulnerable.

The Holy Spirit's forte is helping people who are weak and vulnerable. They simply have to be willing to accept His help.

The winepress was the place where the angel of the Lord found Gideon, where he had been using his gift of threshing wheat in the wrong place, creating more trouble than benefit. The Holy Spirit's desire is that your gift operates efficiently and effectively. In the New Testament, we find references to the Holy Spirit and His delivering power described as new wine. Gideon took his enemy to the place where he had been hiding, where his victory first began, where the angel of the Lord began to confront limitation and weakness in his life, the place where he began to live in God. Living in and being led by the Spirit means that we have found the place where the Spirit of God can confront the limitations of our soul and where we are enabled with supernatural ability to overcome what we could not overcome before. Gideon overcame both his enemies, lack of vision and weakness, through Christ the Rock and His Holy Spirit.

When Gideon was first found by the angel of the Lord, he was not yet a mighty man of valor in his own eyes or by experience—but he had potential. God worked on Gideon's soul by calling him, "you mighty man of valor." Words from God, such as, "Have I not sent you?" "I will be with you," and "You will overcome Midian as one man" transformed Gideon's soul; and in the end, he became the mighty man of valor that God destined him to be.

The Holy Spirit will work with us until God fulfills what He has promised for our lives. Haggai 2:5 says, "According to the word that I covenanted with you when you came out of Egypt, so My Spirit remains among you; do not fear!" The Holy Spirit makes sure that the deal is closed and that the contract, or as the Bible says, "the covenant" is fulfilled. We should not be concerned or afraid of what tomorrow brings as long as we are confident of what the destiny and purpose is that God has for us.

ANOINTED TO WIN

A person who understands and receives his destiny will be a person who is very dangerous to the kingdom of darkness. The kingdom of darkness can do nothing against him, because the Holy Spirit is on the assignment. God gives us a little more information in Isaiah 10:26-27 about how this works:

> And the Lord of hosts will stir up a scourge for him like the slaughter of Midian at the rock of Oreb; as His rod was on the sea, so will He lift it up in the manner of Egypt. It shall come to pass in that day that his burden will be taken away from your shoulder, and his yoke from your neck, and the yoke will be destroyed because of the anointing oil (Isaiah 10:26-27).

Verse 26 says that God will vindicate us from the enemy and then God gives a reference to the kind of victory that we will experience. We will experience a victory over stolen dreams and weakness.

In verse 27, we see a familiar passage that describes the extent of the deliverance and freedom that we can experience. We can expect the Holy Spirit to do three things while bringing deliverance to us. First, God will remove the limitations from our shoulders ("shoulders" represents authority). The enemy wants to steal your authority to achieve, your authority to live freely, and your authority to have success. Second, God will return your liberty. A "yoke on the neck" represents control and the lack of freedom to make decisions. The enemy wants to control you by containing your actions and limiting your freedom. Of course, God will never stand for that. Jesus said, "My yoke is easy and My burden is light" (Mt. 11:30). God doesn't set us free simply to allow us to run free and loose without any restraint. He sets us free and allows us to choose His way, which is an easy and liberating one.

Finally, after taking the enemy's yoke from your neck, God will destroy the yoke because He has anointed you to accomplish something. The anointing oil itself has no empowering quality but the purpose for the anointing does. The oil used is symbolic, and not a potion of any kind. God pours anointing oil on anything or anyone who He has separated for a special purpose for Himself. The anointing oil poured on young David's head, flowing down his face, was a confirmation to everyone who saw him that he was destined to be king.

The anointing oil is a symbol of what God is planning to do with the person who is being anointed. When God makes His plan clear to someone and that person desires to fulfill that plan, God will make His plan happen by any means possible. He will demolish the yoke of the enemy in order to keep you on track. He won't fight for you because of the oil, but He will demolish the yoke because of the purpose for which you are anointed. As we read in First John 2:27, we are anointed with the Holy Spirit who coexists with us for the sake of accomplishing God's purpose and destiny on our lives.

PROTECTING THE INVESTMENT

God has invested interest in you. Consequently, He has sent His Investment Counselor to help you make good decisions and help you walk in proper judgment. In Ezekiel 36:26-27, God makes clear that He must give you a new heart, a new intellect, new feelings, and a new soul.

I will give you a new heart and put a new spirit within you; I will take the heart of stone out of your flesh and give you a heart of flesh. I will put My Spirit within you and cause you to walk in My statutes, and you will keep My judgments and do them (Ezekiel 36:26-27).

God promises to give us a new soul which is the Hebrew word *Leb* (labe): "the heart; used very widely for the feelings, the will and even the intellect; likewise for the center of anything." We can't have success when a hardened or stony heart hampers our decision-making ability. God needs us to have good judgment. To guarantee that we make proper decisions, He has put His Spirit within us to help us make the right choices. Success comes from making the right decisions.

On the other hand, a hardened heart is a heart that no longer yields to its conscience, the part of our soul where we make decisions (see Rom. 2:15). The Holy Spirit must quicken or make alive our conscience because we have been born in sin and have inherited a stony heart. The Holy Spirit works with our conscience to help us know what is right and what is wrong. The Holy Spirit was given to us to help us live the way that God wants us to live.

WORD OF WISDOM FROM YOUR COACH

At this point, I want to revisit a subject that we touched on earlier in this chapter—the authoritative prescription. An authoritative prescription comes from one of the gifts of the Spirit—the word of wisdom. Even though the Holy Spirit can communicate to man through the word of knowledge or the discerning of spirits, the word of wisdom is a unique and powerful problem-solving gift. An authoritative prescription is given to solve problems; authoritative prescriptions are solutions that the Holy Spirit gives us to help us live in unlimited success and favor. (In this book, I address two gifts of the Spirit—word of wisdom and the working of miracles; you can learn more about how to discover and develop the other gifts of the Spirit for daily and practical use in my book, *As the Spirit Wills*.)

The word of wisdom is a gift that finds wise solutions for any problem that may arise. In the book, *The Holy Spirit, My Senior Partner*, Paul Yonggi Cho writes, "Wisdom is the function by which we can effectively use knowledge to solve problems and bring forth blessings and victory." He also writes, "The word of wisdom referred to as a gift of the Holy Spirit is given only supernaturally to a believer who through this wisdom wonderfully solves problems in the difficult circumstances and thereby gives God glory."[1]

When you operate in this gift, you will be able to see solutions to problems that others will be scratching their heads over.

The Holy Spirit will speak wisdom that will meet your needs as long as you approach Him with sincerity and trust. However, He will never cast pearls before swine. He will not continually give wisdom to those who refuse to receive or walk in His wisdom. Wisdom in and of itself cannot create change because wisdom comes in the form of instruction. Heavenly wisdom is the same as any other instruction in that if the instructions are not followed, then the expected end will not come to pass. Please remember this point: The word of wisdom can work its miracle to change circumstances *only* if you obey what the Holy Sprit instructs you to do.

Most of the gifts of the Holy Spirit work in conjunction with another gift. For example, the word of knowledge can operate with the gift of healing, the word of wisdom, or the gift of prophecy. Pastor Benny Hinn, when praying for the sick, will first call out a sickness by the word of knowledge, and then the gift of healing will make it happen. In the same manner, the word of wisdom operates with other gifts of the Holy Spirit. The majority of the time, the word of wisdom will activate the working of miracles.

Before I give you an example from the Bible, I want to give you a greater understanding of what the gift of working of miracles is, by proceeding through a word study. First Corinthians 12:10 reads, "To another the working of miracles, to another prophecy, to another discerning of spirits, to another different kinds of tongues, to another the interpretation of tongues." The word "working" is the Greek word *energema* (en-erg´-ay-mah), meaning "an effect or a result" and the words "of miracles" is the Greek word *dunamis* (doo´-nam-is), meaning "force, miraculous power (usually by implication, a miracle itself)." So, the working of miracles is a gift that releases miraculous power in order to accomplish a certain result. The working of miracles works with the word of wisdom causing the result of whatever the word of wisdom is supposed to bring to pass. For example, consider Matthew 17:24-27:

When they had come to Capernaum, those who received the temple tax came to Peter and said, "Does your Teacher not pay the temple tax?" He said, "Yes." And when he had come into the house, Jesus anticipated him, saying, "What do you think, Simon? From whom do the kings of the earth take customs or taxes, from their sons or from strangers?" Peter said to Him, "From strangers." Jesus said to him, "Then the sons are free. Nevertheless, lest we offend them, go to the sea, cast in a hook, and take the fish that comes up first. And when you have opened its mouth, you will find a piece of money; take that and give it to them for Me and you."

If Peter hadn't obeyed Jesus and gone fishing, he would have never experienced this wonderful miracle. We know that it was a miracle because it is against the odds for a coin to be in a fish's mouth. The problem: unpaid taxes; the solution or the word of wisdom or instruction: go fishing; and the working of miracles: the coin in the fish's mouth used to pay taxes. The word of wisdom doesn't necessarily have to make sense to you, because usually it will speak about possibilities that are beyond the odds. When you receive an authoritative prescription or a creative thought, don't assume that it cannot happen because it is a little far-fetched in your mind or in the mind of others. If God gave it to you, He has already made up His mind that it will come to pass. Creative thoughts come to pass because of the working of miracles. You have divine appointments because of the working of miracles, and you have supernatural opportunities because of the working of miracles. But without a creative thought or an authoritative prescription, you will not receive the workings of miracles. Remember, the Holy Sprit is your helper, and He desires to make you successful.

Once the Holy Spirit has worked on you—confronting your thoughts, standing in your weakness, convincing you of God's destiny, giving you authoritative prescriptions to solve problems in your life and showing you pictures of tomorrow—it's up to you to maintain what you have been given. You do this by keeping your thoughts pure and positive. Positive thinking is God's design; negative thinking is the devil's plan. You can make a choice of whose report you will believe. If you can maintain a positive perspective, you will notice that people and opportunities will be divinely released to you from God.

ENDNOTE

1. Paul Yonggi Cho, *The Holy Spirit, My Senior Partner* (Altamonte Springs, FL: Creation House), 154.

— CHAPTER THREE —

THE MAGNET OF SUCCESS

To the pure, all things are pure, but to those who are corrupt-
ed and do not believe, nothing is pure. In fact, both their
minds and consciences are corrupted (Titus 1:15 NIV).

I woke up frightened one day. Thoughts of *What if?* raced
through my mind. *What if it doesn't work? What if I can't pay my*
bills? What if I can't solve these problems? The most horrific situations moved through my head. The more I thought about them,
the worse things became. I revolved the worst scenarios around
and around in my mind. Then suddenly, a very strong thought
was impressed upon me. It was God's voice saying to me, "If you
continue to have worst-case scenario thinking, then you will attract worst-case scenarios to yourself." This thought gripped me.
I was immediately confronted with the understanding that I was
drawing to myself what I was imagining through my thoughts
and my speech. Instead of trying to maintain a mind-set of possibility, I was imagining only the worst.

Most people relate to their future by their present circumstances. However, between now and your future goal, there is a lot of development and creativity to be experienced. So, it is truly unfair to you and to God to underestimate what could actually happen within a short amount of time that could potentially change your entire existence. New frontiers should be viewed as new opportunities to discover about yourself and God's abilities.

Positive Thinking

You attract to yourself whatever you have created in your mind. Staying positive and maintaining the confidence that all things are possible to those who believe will automatically draw opportunity. Your thoughts do a lot more than fill empty space in your head; they create a belief system for you that you constantly live by.

Ephesians 3:20 says, "Now to Him who is able to do exceedingly abundantly above all that we ask or think, according to the power that works in us." The bigger you think, the bigger God can work on your behalf. We must live in big thoughts if we want to be like Christ. God is not satisfied with answering what you and I request or think because it limits Him. God wants to bless us extravagantly and abundantly even more than we could ask or think. He can do this if our thoughts are at least seeds of possibility. God is not going to do exceedingly above and beyond what we ask or think if we are negative. Negative thought kills your creativity; it locks you into a room of failure. Negativity doesn't give you even a fighting chance to make good out of a terrible situation. You can't exceed negativity because there is nothing to work with. It is not the language of God; it's the language of the devil.

In the book, *The Fourth Dimension*, Dr. Paul Yonggi Cho writes, "Many people think that they will receive just by asking. The Bible, however, says 'ask or *think*.' God gives answers through your thought life, 'exceeding abundantly above all that we ask or think.' What do you think? Do you think poverty? Do you think sickness? Do you think impossibility? If you pray this way, God has no channel through which to flow."[1] Our thoughts induce the power of God to flow in our lives. What do you want to flow in your life? Whatever it is, let it first flow through your thoughts; subsequently, you will see it flow in excess and abundance in your life.

IN THE IMAGE OF GOD

Many people rely on what they think about themselves and the image in which they see themselves, whether it is real or false. If you see yourself as successful in your occupation, you will surely accomplish that vision. If, on the other hand, you have a negative self-image, then you will have a hard time picturing yourself in successful situations and opportunities. Yet, when you see your life according to a God-image, you will see everything as being possible. A God-image allows you to look beyond your faults and into God's ability. Through self-image alone there is the possibility of failure, but with a God-image, you will see your life according to what God thinks about you. A God-image is the revelation that you have been created in His image and likeness. It is the understanding that your abilities or your inabilities cannot add to or take away from your success. Believing that God believes in you will activate the supernatural ability of God that makes all things possible.

God, being a good God, always has good thoughts toward us. Even if you have an incredible self-image, your self-image can never create the kind of possibilities that a God-image can. Our thoughts are not God's thoughts, nor are our ways His ways. God is in Heaven looking at us from a standpoint of perfection, so everything that He desires for us is perfection. This makes His ways higher and His thoughts higher than ours.

The way you see yourself will create a positive or a negative atmosphere around you. If you see things pure, then pure things will come to you; just as effectively, if you see things tainted then you will attract tainted things to you. You are what you think about. Whatever consumes your thoughts, will dominate your life. God desires that we prosper and are healthy. He wants to help you and keep you healthy in all of your business affairs and on the journey of life. Yet, God can help you only if you will embrace His thoughts. God's thoughts are thoughts of hope and prosperity; they are thoughts of good success.

IMAGINE THAT!

We must learn to use our imagination in order to hear from God.

> *"For My thoughts are not your thoughts, nor are your ways My ways," says the Lord. "For as the heavens are higher than the earth, so are My ways higher than your ways, and My thoughts than your thoughts. For as the rain comes down, and the snow from heaven, and do not return there, but water the earth, and make it bring forth and bud, that it may give seed to the sower and bread to the eater"* (Isaiah 55:8-10).

God's imagination or creativity is greater than our imagination and creativity. Our thoughts are not God's thoughts, but we can receive God's thoughts by exercising our imagination and creativity. If we fail to do so, we will limit what God could show us.

Of course, we can't allow our thoughts to run their own course. We must learn to discern the difference between God's thoughts, or our thoughts, and the enemy's suggestions, by submitting our thoughts to God. Proverbs 16:3 says, "Commit your works to the Lord, and your thoughts will be established." If we commit our works and deeds to Christ, our thoughts will be established. Our works then become a direct result of our thought life. God will govern our works if we submit ourselves to Him. We will never commit an act without first having a thought toward that action. Our actions don't just simply come from nowhere; our actions come from our thought life. You can keep your thoughts healthy, holy, and success based, and when you do so, you will keep your actions healthy, holy, and successful.

THE TONGUE—A LIFE OR DEATH MATTER

The power of creation and destruction is also in your mouth, and you daily create success or you cause destruction according to what you speak. You may or may not be aware of this power, and you may believe that something like the New Age movement created this principle; but the truth is, you have created what you are today, by what you have been thinking and speaking. God has given you the power to fill yourself with life or death by what you put in your mouth. The sooner you reconcile yourself to the fact that you control your future by what is in your mouth, the sooner you will run to God for help with your speech. Not only can this power destroy your future when it is used improperly, but it can destroy people around you. Creative thoughts are brought to life by the positive words that we say. In addition, creative thoughts die by the negative speech we allow to proceed from our mouth.

It is amazing how a huge ship can be steered by a small rudder; likewise, your life is steered by your tongue. I often hear people talk, who have a hard time controlling their conversation. You know, the people who say whatever they want, whenever they want, tactlessly, without forethought, without a conscience or consideration toward the people around them. I have heard them say, "I'm sorry, I just can't help myself. I have to be myself." When a person can't control his tongue, he reveals that he is like a city without protective walls and his enemy is on his way to destroy him. Proverbs 25:28 makes this clear: "Whoever has no rule over his own spirit is like a city broken down, without walls." This kind of attitude will destroy the person as well as everyone around them, so beware of your conversation and the conversation of those around you. Just as you cannot have salt water and fresh water pour from the same water source, neither can you have gossip and words of encouragement from the same mouth. You cannot utter blessing and cursing. The tongue releases the issues of life, or it releases the issues of death. The tongue builds you or hangs you. Make provision for your success by keeping a positive attitude and speaking only of possibility.

A common negative phrase often used is "I am just being realistic." Well, if you desire to remain in the "real world," you will not be able to possess heavenly favor, because faith has nothing to do with present realities. You have to learn to write your destiny by what you say. If you continue to play the devil's advocate, he may think you are on his team and start hanging out with you. Proverbs 18:21 says, "Death and life are in the power of the tongue, and those who love it will eat its fruit." What does it mean to say, "power is in the tongue"? Your words are creative, and they create atmospheres around you. If you talk like the devil, then you will find the devil and his friends gathered around you. If you talk like God, then you will experience God and all of His goodness. God created everything with His mouth, and as His children we create everything in our sphere of influence with our mouths.

It is important to protect your destiny by keeping yourself from speaking negatively. King David, one of the great kings of Israel, prayed for God to protect him from his enemy by putting a guard before his mouth. The words that we speak will govern our future. Your destiny is created by words. God created the heavens and the earth through what He spoke. According to the Bible, there was nothing created that was not first spoken. Your thoughts cannot be creative without the words to back them.

THE COMPANY YOU KEEP

I am convinced that how you think and what you say create a kind of magnetic field around you or some kind of funky atmosphere. Consider the little boy Pig Pen from the cartoon "Charley Brown," who is always so dirty you can actually see the dirt cloud surrounding him. And whenever you come in contact with Pig Pen, his swirling dirt cloud also gets all over you. I don't think that Pig Pen's cloud would be offensive to dirty people, but for clean people who are trying to stay clean, it would be repelling.

Have you ever heard the statements, "You're judged by the company you keep" or "Birds of a feather flock together"? Have you ever seen a bald eagle in all of its majesty hanging around noisy and obnoxious crows? Of course not. Yet many of us desiring to be eagles continue to spend our time with crows. We hang out with Pig Pen, the dirt-cloud boy, while at the same time, we want to be clean. I personally like to be around people who are positive thinkers and speakers. Your thoughts and speech attract to you natural things as well as spiritual.

Believing in the Unseen

(As it is written, "I have made you a father of many nations") in the presence of Him whom he believed—God, who gives life to the dead and calls those things which do not exist as though they did (Romans 4:17).

We must get used to calling those things that are not as though they are. This is not just some "blab it, grab it" stuff. This is the key to the existence of everything. Everything that exists started with someone seeing, believing, and speaking. Doubt, negativity, and unbelief when spoken from your mouth, will create circumstances and make the things that God wants to do in your life impossible. Faith, hope, joy, and possibility thinking, as Dr. Robert Schuler calls it, creates an opportunity for God and his angels to work on your behalf.

Endnote

1. Paul Yonggi Cho, *The Fourth Dimension* (South Plainfield, NJ: Bridge Publishing, Inc., 1979), 149-150.

— CHAPTER FOUR —

SUCCESS—A SOUL ISSUE

And have put on the new self, which is being renewed in knowledge in the image of its Creator (Colossians 3:10 NIV).

WHAT IS THE SOUL?

The soul is a mystery. It is not like the body that has been dissected and researched for centuries, and of which we know and understand much of its function and potential. And it is not like our spirit, wherein we understand our spirit came from God and will return to God. We do know that our soul houses our mind, feelings, emotions, thoughts, and I am sure much more. Each year, science discovers more and more about the soul.

The soul of man is where the Spirit of God communicates. The soul is the entrance to the spirit of man, whether he is saved or unsaved. Of course, our spirit man receives information from the Spirit of God, but it is of noneffect until it has become a part of your soul.

For the last ten years, I have seen prophetically and have spoken prophetically to saved and unsaved people around the world. After analyzing the results, I have determined that those individuals who allowed the personal prophetic word of the Lord to become a part of their soul—a part of their thoughts, feelings, and emotions—were the ones who consistently saw fulfillments to those personal prophetic words.

The same thing occurs in the realm of healing. When we pray for the sick, the greatest results occur for the ones who actually see themselves delivered and envision what their life will be like once they are totally healed. God can give us breakthroughs, but our soul's capacity is the thing that helps us receive, keep, and maintain these breakthroughs.

TRUE SUCCESS

At this point I want to take a brief moment and bring success into perspective for you. I did not write this book because I think that success is the most important thing in the world. I believe what is of upmost importance is that on the day you stand before the Lord, He will know you and recognize Himself in you and receive you with open arms.

> Not everyone who says to Me, "Lord, Lord," shall enter the kingdom of heaven, but he who does the will of My Father in heaven. Many will say to Me in that day, "Lord, Lord, have we not prophesied in Your name, cast out demons in Your name, and done many wonders in Your name?" And then I will declare to them, "I never knew you; depart from Me, you who practice lawlessness!" (Matthew 7:21-23)

Here we see that if we neglect our own soul and live like a devil behind closed doors, it really won't matter to God if we do great things for Him and operate in the gifts of the Spirit. At the same time, if you do pursue a relationship with the Lord and a life holy and pleasing to Him but neglect the gifts you have received from Him, you fall short of His plan for you as well. In

Matthew chapter 25, we read that the Lord does not want us to hide our talents, but multiply them, which requires creative thought on our part from the Lord. There is no way you can ever be a blessing to others the way God expects you to be if you perpetually experience failure in your life. God desires success for you as a vehicle for everything He plans to do through you.

LET'S CLARIFY SOME MISUNDERSTANDINGS

This book is designed to help you condition your soul for the success that God has reserved for you. I promise you it is greater than what the world has ever seen! The only way you can have success is through the development of your soul. That is one thing that we have misunderstood in Christianity. Many of us have been taught that we "finally arrived" as soon as we became spiritually born again. Consequently, we have completely neglected the next step—the development of our soul. We have been trying for years to live through our spirit, without developing our soul.

It can be likened to people who win the lottery. They never did anything to earn the money, nor did they develop any qualities to obtain the wealth. So even while they have access to the money, they have no ability to manage the money. Before long, there is nothing left because there was nothing in their soul in the first place to control such enormous capacity. Sometimes we want to negate the process without understanding that the process makes the success all the more enjoyable. If you study the history of lottery winners, you will find very few who have prepared for success, resulting in temporary fulfillment and long-term disappointment. Spending their money without preparation and planning, they are left with nothing because they ultimately sabotage themselves.

It's the same principle in the Body of Christ. We have been so gift driven, that we've neglected to emphasize a person's soul and character. Yet the soul is where the character of God manifests itself, where the fruit of the Spirit manifests. Our gifts should not be the focal point of our success; rather our integrity and character must be.

Donald Trump has a soul and Billy Graham has a soul. As I am writing this book, Donald Trump is not a Christian and Billy Graham is a mighty man of God, yet both men are successful in their own sphere. Now let me ask you this: If the *spirit* of a person is the key to his success, how can Donald Trump be so successful? I know many of you reading this may be saying, "Yeah, but he's not a Christian, so does he really have success?" Remember that success is relevant to the person who is pursuing it. In the natural terms of success, Donald Trump is successful, simply because he has determined what he wants and has accomplished it. That is success! You make up in your soul what the desire of your heart is and then you go after it with all of your heart, soul, and strength—whether your success is having a loving family, owning a nice house with a white picket fence, traveling to the mission field to plant churches, or becoming a multimillionaire. You set the level for success based upon what you believe you are destined to do and accomplish here on the earth.

I would be hard-pressed to say that Donald Trump would be doing something different than what he is doing now if he was a Christian. Success is a heart issue, success is a soul issue, success is an emotion issue, success is a thought issue, and success can only be accomplished through biblical principles. What do I mean? I mean that even though a person may not have the godly character that the Bible talks about, he can still live in and embrace divine principles that are clearly seen in the Bible. God's laws are universal laws that cannot be disturbed by the absence of salvation. Universal laws that create success will create success whether you are perfect or not. For instance, seedtime and harvest is a universal law that has no prejudice. The ground does not consider a farmer as saved or unsaved. The seed and ground do not judge a farmer to see if he is a good man or not. Sowing and reaping is a universal law that God has created, and if you learn to work within these laws, you will become a successful farmer.

And so, we can conclude that success can be achieved without salvation, but success doesn't last forever without salvation. My point is simple: As a Christian, you must not neglect the development of your soul because your success is dependent upon how you process your destiny, how you process your life, and how you process God's promises for your future. We so quickly label things as being "soulish" and therefore reject them as if God did not create the soul as well. Often we reject these things without asking God for wisdom and guidance, hence we cut our potential short. How unfortunate.

YOU WILL HAVE HELP

Just as God informed Joshua that He wanted him to have great success, God is interested in prospering us and making us successful as well. John, one of the apostles, wrote in Third John 1:2: "Beloved, I pray that you may prosper in all things and be in health, just as your soul prospers." This verse is rich! John has been praying for the readers to prosper. It is all right to pray for prosperity; it's okay to ask God to bless you. However, John was not just praying for them to have money or a new house, although there is nothing wrong with having those things. He was asking for something much more valuable. He was praying for them to have help on their road to success. Yes, the original Greek text reveals to us that John used the word *euodoo* (yoo-od-o´-o) for "may prosper" which means, "to help on the road, succeed in reaching, or to succeed in business affairs." He was not just saying, "Be happy, don't worry, live long, and prosper." He was saying, "I am praying for you on the road to success, and I am praying that God will send you help as you go." God not only wants you to have success, but He will send you the proper help and guidance as you go. First and foremost, the Helper, the Holy Spirit, will be with you; and secondly, God will send you the right people—divine appointments.

Prosperity was not the only thing that John prayed for; he also said, "and be in health." He prayed that God would give them success without corruption, for their spirit, soul, and body. Why should we have success just to lose it? Proverbs 10:22 says, "The blessing of the Lord makes one rich, and He adds no sorrow with it." Whatever we receive in Christ is not subject to destruction.

SUCCESS STARTS IN YOUR SOUL

For years I read Third John 1:2, never realizing what I needed to do in order to live in the prosperity and health that John was praying for. Maybe I had so much selfish ambition that I couldn't see it. Then all of a sudden, one day when I was reading the words "just as your soul prospers," it jumped off the page. There it was—the secret to success, the science of success, and the psychology of success. Prosperity and success starts in the soul. That is the exact reason that the unsaved can also have such great prosperity and great success. They spend most of their time developing their soul because that's where they live—in their soul. As Christians, we focus most of our attention on our spiritual authority, not realizing that the health of our soul can hinder or increase our spiritual authority. I am not saying that we need to neglect our spiritual growth. I am merely saying that many Christians have not conditioned their souls to be healthy in order to obtain success and prosperity. I know there are unsaved people who are very balanced and relatively healthy in their soul. They are loving to their family, they demonstrate respect for their closest friends, and seem to control their appetites very well. These are people who are relatively successful, and they usually accomplish what they set out to do. Then there are Christians who are very spiritual in their conversation and even have ministries that touch the nations; yet their children are afraid of them, their wives don't know when they might explode again, they are completely out of control when it comes to food and drink, and are basically unpleasant to be around. My point is, the soul of man is in need of extensive work, even after he receives salvation, especially if he never had godly parents who trained him well. Your soul will lean to whichever is stronger—either the flesh or the spirit. Nevertheless, if you are both spiritually strong and sound in your mind, emotions, feelings, and thinking, all the hindrances and stops will be removed.

A TRANSFORMED SOUL PLEASING TO GOD

Everything that God has fashioned grows, reproduces, and multiplies in some way. Scientific researchers say that our body's entire cellular system renews itself every seven years. We know as Christians that our spirit is renewed daily. Second Corinthians 4:16 says, "Therefore we do not lose heart. Even though our outward man is perishing, yet the inward man is being renewed day by day." The Word of God is very clear that our mind or soul must be renewed. We see this most clearly in Romans 12:2: "And do not be conformed to this world, but be transformed by the renewing of your mind, that you may prove what is that good and acceptable and perfect will of God." The end result is to prove what is good, acceptable, and the predetermined desire of God. The goal is not to be transformed; the goal is to please God. And the only way we can fulfill His desire is to think like He thinks.

Ever since mankind received the fallen nature after the fall of Adam and Eve, we all have been born in sin, and even though our spirits are renewed after we receive Jesus as our Savior, our mind is unchanged until we decide to change it. We don't naturally think like God, but we can develop the same desires that He has, and consequently those desires will cause us to change. In order to change, we must develop discipline. It is hard to motivate change just for the sake of change. A person must have a desire, which is the only thing that can bring change. And in order to obtain desire, you must begin with an emotion that causes desire, such as hope, joy, greed, fear, or lust.

The Bible is very clear in these verses that you must not be conformed to this world but be transformed by the renewing of your mind. That also means that you should not allow unhealthy emotions to rule your life such as fear, lust, greed, or jealousy. These emotions are worldly and not the good, acceptable, and perfect will of God. Our pattern of living is different when we become Christians; we are not to "be conformed" to this world, meaning we are not to try to *suschematizo* (soos-khay-mat-id´-zo), which means "to be fashioned alike or to conform to the same pattern." The worldly pattern is a lesser pattern than what God has fashioned us for. A pattern is something that you base your life, your family, your belief system, your business practices, your future, and your purpose on. If you have an unhealthy pattern, you will definitely have unhealthy results.

Who are you patterning yourself after and whom are you following? If you don't like what you see, you'd better change your pattern because you will become exactly like the pattern that you are following whether you like it or not.

We see it all the time. People grow up saying, "I will never be like my father, like my mother, like my brother," and so on— only to look in the mirror 20 years later and discover that they have become that very person. Why? Because the only way you can change one pattern is by intentionally adopting another pattern which you become very passionate about. Changing a pattern cannot be done with passive hopes and dreams. You must despise the one and strongly desire the other. If Christ passionately becomes your pattern, then you are guaranteed that you will develop a healthy pattern and live in the good, acceptable, and the perfect determination of God.

TIME, DELIVERANCE, AND EMPOWERMENT

Transformation is not an overnight miracle, no matter how much we desire it. It is a process of time, deliverance, and empowerment. Just as it took years of sinful generations to create the unhealthy patterns, it will also take time to transform them into healthy patterns—not because God cannot miraculously change you; it simply takes time to know and understand all the benefits that are in Christ. When I was first saved, I didn't understand healing, nor did I know that someone could be healed. But once I saw God heal someone, it created a strong desire in my heart to see it again and experience it for myself. I began to pray for many people after that, and yet they didn't get healed. Why? Was it because God doesn't heal? No! But because I needed to develop a greater understanding of God, of why He heals, of faith, of resistance, of unbelief, of confession, and the list can go on and on. I needed time to develop my soul in that area. Time is what everyone needs.

I also needed deliverance—deliverance from myself and from old habits. Old habits will not die easily on their own, but in God they die as soon as you choose to let them go in order to get a hold of something better. The faster you let your old man go, the sooner God can lift up the new man in you. Most of our problems are not other people; most of our problems are found within ourselves. And the biggest mistake we could every make is to ignore them and hope they will change on their own.

Empowerment is necessary after you are delivered from yourself. Empowerment means that you know who you are, what you can do and that you have the open door to move forward. Empowerment also means that you don't have to wait for approval from anyone to possess what God is giving you.

It would be easier if we could have everything we wanted without changing. It would be easier to accomplish everything that God has designed for us without transforming, but to have the best, it always demands becoming better. We must become better thinkers. Our thoughts formulate every action. We must be renewed in our mind. We can't have a half mental change, but we must change fully. The Greek word for this change is *anakainosis*, meaning "renovation, a complete change for the better." God wants us to be better people, better mothers, better fathers, better ministers, better businesspeople, whatever we do and whatever we are passionate about. We must become whole in our minds in order to achieve the best.

Sometimes I watch a television show called "This Old House." The creative and informative program shows you step-by-step what to do if you are planning to renovate your own home. This is what the Spirit of God does for us—He shows us who we can be, using Christ as the pattern and shows us step by step how to renovate ourselves.

The renovation of your mind will help you test and approve what is right and wrong, what is good or bad, acceptable or unacceptable, what is a distraction or the perfect will of God. Your future success is based upon your ability to properly judge your options. These decisions should not be made through worldly or carnal perspectives. You can't afford to rest your future on sensual or undirected emotions.

OVERCOMING A LIFE OF LUST

> *How they told you that there would be mockers in the last time who would walk according to their own ungodly lusts. These are sensual persons, who cause divisions, not having the Spirit. But you, beloved, building yourselves up on your most holy faith, praying in the Holy Spirit* (Jude 1:18-20).

Jude describes "soulish" people as people who walk in their own ungodly lusts. Ungodliness stems from our own lusts. Because of the fall of man, we naturally live in sensuality. A sensual person doesn't live according to the laws of God, spiritually or legally. He is a lawless person. He lives only for fulfillment of his own appetites. Charles Finney in *Systematic Theology* says that man has a moral obligation to live above the sensual nature of man. The sensual nature of man is ungoverned and lives only by instincts, just like an animal. The animal and bestial nature of man rules his own life because he doesn't have the Holy Spirit to govern or guide him. The word that Jude uses for sensual is a word that means animate.

Jude says that those people who are sensual cause division because they aren't filled with the Spirit. No wonder marriages fail, churches split, and families feud—the Spirit of God is not leading every party that is involved. Sensual people have only in-stinctive decision-making capabilities. They don't make deci-sions that benefit everyone; they make decisions that benefit themselves. They are satisfied only by lust.

Jude gives a solution for overcoming the sensual nature of man. Even though you are saved and possibly filled with the Holy Spirit, you must obey what you receive when He speaks, in order to overcome the natural desires that you fight. You can overcome the natural man by building yourself up on your most holy *faith*. We have already visited how to do this in the chapter on the Holy Spirit. When you pray in the Spirit, the Holy Spirit begins to speak mysteries that proceed from the throne of God regarding your future and purpose.

The next question is: How do I increase in faith? Romans 10:17 says that faith comes by hearing, and hearing comes by the Word of God. So if you are going to grow in faith, you must first grow in hearing. When you pray in the Spirit, the Holy Spirit shows you who you are in Christ. With every revelation of Jesus, with every revelation of His goodness, with every revelation of His power, and with every revelation of His character, the Holy Sprit builds the attributes of Christ into your life. If you receive the understanding that Christ is patient, then the Holy Spirit be-gins to build upon you the revelation of patience that we have noticed in Christ. The words "build up" are actually *epoikodomeo*, which means, "to build upon, to build up; to finish the structure of which the foundation has already been laid, to give constant increase in Christian knowledge and in a life conformed thereto." This definition is from the Thayer's Greek Dictionary. This is an awesome revelation! This means that the foundation of animalistic and bestial nature that I have been living by, is no longer my foundation, but Jesus' life is now my foundation; and the more revelation that I receive about Jesus, the more I am transformed into Christ's likeness. This is the likeness we want if we want to achieve success that lasts.

Rely on the Holy Spirit

Romans chapter 1 reveals to us that the spirit of holiness has been sent by God to help us live holy; however, the Holy Spirit cannot help anyone who will not recognize His help. If we purposefully neglect to give God glory, then we will be given over to our own lusts. Romans 1:28 says, "And even as they did not like to retain God in their knowledge, God gave them over to a reprobate mind, to do those things which are not fitting." We must recognize God as being God in order to be delivered from ourselves.

The natural man has no place in God, because the natural man rejects God. We see this clearly in First Corinthians 2:14-15: "But the natural man does not receive the things of the Spirit of God, for they are foolishness to him; nor can he know them, because they are spiritually discerned. But he who is spiritual judges all things, yet he himself is rightly judged by no one." We can change the way we think. The natural man doesn't have to stay natural; he can become spiritual. But unlike those who practice a worldly spirituality, we must depend on the Spirit of God in order to be spiritual. In other religions, a man can ascend to a higher consciousness. In Christianity, our higher consciousness is found only through reliance on the conscience of the Holy Spirit. Without the help of the Holy Spirit the natural man thinks that the things of God are foolish. It's foolishness to him because we must exalt God and die to ourselves in order to become more spiritual. A Christian spiritually develops through the Holy Spirit and not through his own consciousness.

The devil told Adam and Eve that they could know the difference between good and evil. In the pursuit for knowledge of good and evil, they lost their connection with God. Our reliance on the Holy Spirit and our faith in the salvation of Jesus Christ is the only way that we can be reconnected or joined to God. Our spirit is awakened when we receive Christ, but our soul gets restored only through renewing our mind and through reliance on God.

If the enemy can keep influencing your thoughts, heart, and mind, he can keep you in failure. He does everything that He can to keep you confused, distracted, fearful, and doubting. The only way that you can guard your thoughts, heart, and mind is by living in peace. When you rely on God for everything, you will experience peace no matter what your circumstances may be. A spiritual man lives in peace because he refuses to live according to his own understanding, but according to the things of God.

> *Be anxious for nothing, but in everything by prayer and supplication, with thanksgiving, let your requests be made known to God; and the peace of God, which surpasses all understanding, will guard your hearts and minds through Christ Jesus* (Philippians 4:6-7).

Peace is the sentinel of our hearts and minds.

> *You will keep him in perfect peace, whose mind is stayed on You, because he trusts in You* (Isaiah 26:3).

Peace comes from keeping your eyes on Christ, from trusting in God and not in ourselves.

YOU CAN CHOOSE TO CHANGE

A major ingredient in a healthy soul is the ability to make quality decisions and stick with them. Whether we believe it or not, God has given us the power of choice. Consider Deuteronomy 30:19: "I call heaven and earth as witnesses today against you, that I have set before you life and death, blessing and cursing; therefore choose life, that both you and your descendants may live." If you choose life, you *will* receive life, not only for you, but also for your family and your descendants. If you choose blessing, you *will* receive blessing for you and your family.

Heaven and earth is a witness that God has given everyone the opportunity to live in success. But success will most likely never come to you unless you *choose* it. Success is not based upon where we have been raised nor who our parents are, even though those things do make success a little easier to acquire. We are not limited to the success that our family has experienced or has not experienced. Success is a choice, just as life is a choice, just as receiving Jesus is a choice.

Jesus will not force you to conform to Him. It is your choice to put on Christ. And when you put on Christ, you put on His character—this ensures success, guaranteed!

HOPE!

The character of Christ keeps us from making provision for the flesh and for failure. We will not fulfill the lust of the flesh as long as we are pursuing Christ (see Rom. 13:14). "This hope we have as an anchor of the soul, both sure and steadfast, and which enters the Presence behind the veil" (Heb. 6:19). Christ is our hope and hope is the anchor of our soul. As Christians we gain hope in what we do not yet have, through the Word of God and the spoken word. Hope is the foundation of faith and faith keeps us moving forward and dreaming. Without hope we would stop living. Christ wants us to believe in the best and hope for the best. Hope keeps us from depression and defeat. If a person has hope, it doesn't matter how many times he fails, he will keep on trying until he receives what he has been hoping for.

It's only when our hope gets deferred that our heart and mind become sick. Consequently, a sick soul is not able to make successful decisions. Fortunately, hope keeps our soul from becoming sick. We cannot gain our hope from things or people. We must find our hope in God, and once we receive what we have desired, it becomes a tree of life. A tree produces fruit year after year, and the fruit produces seeds that create more and more trees. Proverbs 13:12 says, "Hope deferred makes the heart sick, but when the desire comes, it is a tree of life." What does this mean? It means that what God accomplishes in your life will not end but will perpetuate. It will continue from your generation to the next generation. I believe that we all want such success in our life that will continue for years to come.

You can create hope by thinking and dreaming of things that you do not have, and you must use your imagination in order to maintain hope. Hope is dreaming of something that doesn't currently exist. Romans 8:24-25 says, "For we were saved in this hope, but hope that is seen is not hope; for why does one still hope for what he sees? But if we hope for what we do not see, we eagerly wait for it with perseverance." If you have what you have been hoping for, then you no longer have to hope for it. If you can see it, there is no longer a need for hope. Hope is what we do not yet see with our natural eyes; it is seeing with our spiritual eyes. Hope is what the spy who entered into the Promised Land brought back—samples of what was to come. The samples were designed to keep them believing and persevering through the storms and the giants. Hope keeps our ship anchored even though the storm rages and the waves of life crash against us. We cannot be moved because our soul is anchored in hope. We simply need to taste the sample of tomorrow's grapes or take a sip of tomorrow's milk and our hope is charged again.

CHAPTER FIVE

PIONEER PITFALLS

But if the Lord creates a new thing, and the earth opens its mouth and swallows them up with all that belongs to them, and they go down alive into the pit, then you will understand that these men have rejected the Lord (Number 16:30).

DISCERNING THE VOICES

Any success I have experienced in my life must be accredited to listening to the right voices. Four different voices will speak to you, and it is necessary that you learn to discern the difference between each of them.

The Voice of God

God's voice is distinct and discernable as a loving and caring voice, even when He is rebuking and correcting. The Bible is very clear that the love of God brings us to repentance.

God speaks through various means, including a still small voice, the Word of God, circumstances, prophetic words, and people. To ensure the authenticity of His voice, we should always filter what we hear through the written Word of God, the Bible. If anything that you hear is contrary to the Word of God or contrary to the character of Christ, it cannot be of God. God's voice will never leave you afraid, shamed, or condemned. Even conviction is liberating and shameless. Romans 8:1 says, "There is therefore now no condemnation to those who are in Christ Jesus, who do not walk according to the flesh, but according to the Spirit." Condemnation is not God's plan for your life. Rather, God's voice confronts your conscience and confirms His goodness. God's voice should draw you closer to Jesus. God wants to communicate with each and every one of us—we just need to listen.

The Voice of the Devil

The devil, on the other hand, is a liar and the father of all lies. His sole desire is to separate you from the will of God. His relationship with man started with a lie, and I am sure it will end with a lie. His words bring condemnation, confusion, shame, doubt, and unbelief.

Satan's words keep us from identifying with Christ, and when heeded, his words bring destruction. The voice of satan will steal, kill, and destroy. When you hear it, you will feel like giving up. As the accuser of the brethren, his voice will make you feel like a failure. His voice is the direct opposite of God's voice, and nothing good comes from it. Actually, the enemy contradicts everything God says. I have made a rule that when I hear the devil's voice, I can say the exact opposite and be comforted by those words as a prophecy. In other words, the devil hears what God says about you and sadistically turns those words into something evil, destructive, and frightening. However, we know that God would never speak anything destructive against us. We can be assured that the enemy knows exactly what good things

God has said about us, and we can embrace the exact opposite of his lies.

For example, when John the Baptist baptized Jesus, a voice came from Heaven and said to Jesus, "This is My beloved Son in whom I am well pleased" (Mt. 3:17b). The first words that came out of the devil's mouth when he met with Jesus were, "*If* You are the Son of God..." (Mt. 4:3b, emphasis mine). His nature questions and contradicts everything that God says. Even when He uses the Scriptures to prove a point, he "twists and turns" it, and misquotes it. He doesn't want you to believe that you can become the person God wants you to become. God's voice always builds identity, while the devil's voice always destroys it.

The Voice of Others

It is even more difficult to discern if the voice of our friends, family members, and associates is the right voice to listen to, because even though these people usually want the best for us, their good intentions are not necessarily God's intentions. So often I hear of people who are feuding with loved ones because they listened to the wrong advice from loving and well-meaning people. Even these voices should be judged by the Word of God and the Spirit of God.

I strongly posture myself when I receive prophetic words or advice from others. First, I check that voice against the Word of God, and then I seek a second opinion. That second opinion must come from a totally neutral and unbiased source who knows nothing about the issue. I keep my thoughts to myself until I get the second opinion. Sometimes I have even waited for a third or a fourth opinion.

It is always better to remain safe than sorry, simply because you must make sure that there are no selfish motivations when it comes to closely related people. Their advice or instruction must be free from manipulation, jealousy, and envy. If they don't display the character of God in all parts of their lives, my advice would be to wait for a second or third opinion from God. If they have a tendency to manipulate in any area of their life, I would be very careful. Be especially careful when others start to gossip. Remember, if they gossip with you about someone else, you can be assured they will gossip with someone else about you.

Your Own Voice

Your own voice will speak very loud, and you will often speak to yourself from the perspective of past and present wounds, hurts, disappointments, and frustrations, unless you have been completely healed. Why? Because you simply want to keep from being hurt again.

Your past acts as a filter in your soul. Everything that you hear, see, smell, feel, and taste brings up a memory in order to help you describe what you are presently experiencing. It also can be described as a reference library. How do you feel or what do you think about when you see a picture of President Kennedy or Elvis? If you were alive when you heard of their deaths, you automatically remember where you were when you heard about the tragedies and what you were doing. Dramatic events always create a reference point, and usually that reference point will direct your thoughts from that point on. An abused person automatically refers back to the person who abused them when they see someone who reminds them of that person, even though that person within their sight is not abusive. Sadly, the filter of an abused soul can affect a new and caring relationship because the voice of the past begins to speak louder then the present reality. The filters in our mind cause spiritual, emotional, and physical reactions, and in the end steers our lives. We often view tomorrow through yesterday's memories.

This becomes a problem when we start to relate to our future through strongholds or filters of failure from our past. Our future is then limited based on the failures of our past. We must break these strongholds before they destroy any possibility of success. I will deal more with strongholds at the end of this chapter.

THE DESTRUCTION OF DIVINE RELATIONSHIPS

It is also of the utmost importance to learn to discern and respect God-given relationships. God often puts people together because they can accomplish greater things together rather than separately. Unfortunately, their egos and personalities often get in the way. Imagine what good could have been accomplished if Paul and Barnabas would have worked out their differences (see Acts 15:35-41). Someone always loses in personality conflicts and disagreements, especially when God is trying to marry two gifts together for the benefit of the Kingdom. Because of the disagreement between Paul and Barnabas, we never hear anything further that Barnabas accomplished for the Kingdom. What's even worse—Mark, who was the cause of the argument, later joined Paul on mission trips, even though the original argument was about Paul not wanting Mark to join his trip with Barnabas. Someone always loses when we can't walk in the covenants that God has ordained in Heaven.

We cannot afford to think that every match made in Heaven will be easy. Sometimes, simply because God has ordained it, it will be difficult. The devil doesn't want agreement on earth, because wherever there is agreement on earth, it is also established in Heaven. We must learn to discern who has been sent to us and whom we are sent to. Breaking up important relationships because of personal differences is not worth the adverse effect it can have on the Kingdom of God, our families, and all the people who are directly involved.

Offenses are pitfalls that can destroy a relationship in no time, and most bad relationships turned sour because an offense occurred. We should never allow offense to end our relationships; however, when it happens, it is very important to win back offended people. In the majority of cases, offenses come from misunderstandings that could be easily solved if only there would be additional or clearer communication. But unfortunately, in many cases, once the misunderstanding ball starts rolling, the enemy plunges in and creates a worse scenario than it should have ever become.

We read in Proverbs 18:19 that, "A brother offended is harder to win than a strong city, and contentions are like the bars of a castle." It is not impossible to win someone's heart who has been offended, but it is very difficult. But...just because it is hard doesn't mean that we shouldn't try. We are held responsible for attempting to restore relationships. If the offended person refuses to reconcile with us, we can move on with a clear conscience.

A Scripture difficult to understand is Matthew 18:7: "Woe to the world because of offenses! For offenses must come, but woe to that man by whom the offense comes!" Why must offenses come? That's the question I would ask every time I would read that verse. After some research and prayer, I began to under stand that the emphasis of this verse is set on the words "must come." I researched those words and found that a better interpretation would be "constraint, distress, and needs cause offenses." All these words are found in the Greek meaning of the words "must come," which describe that offenses need some form of framework to adhere to. If there is no framework of constraint or control, then offenses can never enter into the relationship. If there is no framework of distress, stress, or strain, then offenses cannot be maintained in the relationship. If there is no framework of neediness or want, then there is no reason for offense to enter into a healthy relationship.

Control, stress, and neediness are frames of thinking that unhealthy relationships are based upon. They are the doorways to offenses. If you take care to keep these doors closed in your relationships, you will never have to deal with the invasion of offenses in your life.

The Greek word for "offenses" from the Strong's Dictionary is *skandalon* (skan´-dal-on) (scandal)—"a trap-stick (bent sapling), i.e. snare (figuratively, cause of displeasure or sin)." An offense is a setup, it's a trap, it's a scandal. Offenses come from a third party, meaning, the enemy plays tricks and sets up scenarios and scandals to cause us to think certain things which will create false images in our imagination. The enemy is a predator; he is on the hunt seeking whom he may devour by causing jealousy, envy, or bitterness in the heart.

The enemy will do anything to snare up God-given and God-ordained relationships. How many times have you felt something strange about someone and you then start to imagine that he or she doesn't like you anymore or that they are talking about you? When you talk to them later, you find out that they were just having a bad day and their attitude that day had nothing at all to do with you.

COVENANT RELATIONSHIPS

Covenants create success and protect godly relationships. Success is accomplished when your strengths benefit someone else's weakness and someone else's strengths benefit your weakness. This is true in business, ministry, marriage, and any other place where success can be established. God's system for success demands that I work with someone else. *Isolation* and *independence* are negative words in the Kingdom of God. When the enemy finds you alone, he can fill your head with all types of imaginary things that will cause damage to your life and the life of others.

Covenant relationships aren't based on control, stress, or neediness. Covenant partners understand that they need their relationships. Covenant keepers are givers; they are not in the covenant relationship in order to take advantage of the covenant. When a person of covenant has a need, he can run to his refuge and receive whatever he needs. Covenant people don't try to control each other; they work to liberate each other. In the book, *Renewing the Mind*, Casey Treat writes, "Most people build a circle of friends that help them stay where they are in life and not make changes. They endorse each other's complacency, and encourage each other to stay the same. If one person tries to break out of the rut, the others pressure them not to move on, lest they be left behind. There is a kind of group pressure that stops growth. To renew the mind and go on in life, you must leave friends like these and develop new relationships. A real friend will not slow you down but help you grow and go on in life."[1]

Although Cain and Abel were brothers, they were not covenant partners. Remember that a covenant partnership is one where you use your strengths to help someone else and another's strengths help your weaknesses. When a person of covenant is troubled or stressed out, he can go to his covenant partner who will help him to be set free.

> *Then she bore again, this time his brother Abel. Now Abel was a keeper of sheep, but Cain was a tiller of the ground. And in the process of time it came to pass that Cain brought an offering of the fruit of the ground to the Lord. Abel also brought of the firstborn of his flock and of their fat. And the Lord respected Abel and his offering, but He did not respect Cain and his offering. And Cain was very angry, and his countenance fell. So the Lord said to Cain, "Why are you angry? And why has your countenance fallen?"* (Genesis 4:2-6)

In verse 5 we see that God did not respect the offering of Cain, but in the previous verse He did respect the offering of Abel. Does this mean God was a respecter of persons? No. God was pleased with Abel's offering. Remember that the Bible says the life is in the blood. God was not rejecting Cain; He was rejecting a lifeless sacrifice. There was no blood in his offering; thus, there was no life in his offering.

As an offering, the fruit of the ground brought no pleasure to God. Obviously, God had already set up a system for offering; otherwise, He would have been unjust to judge Cain's offering in such a way. In addition, Cain knew better than to bring just anything to God. If Cain had really wanted to please God, he would have become a covenant partner with his brother and traded some animals for the fruit of the ground. This would have taken care of each of their needs. Cain could have used an offering of blood and Abel would have used some fruit from the ground to eat. All that happens next stems from the understanding that they were not covenant partners as they should have been.

DO RIGHT OR FALL INTO THE TRAP

If you do well, will you not be accepted? And if you do not do well, sin lies at the door. And its desire is for you, but you should rule over it (Genesis 4:7).

The statement, "If you do well" refers to something that Cain knew to do but did not do. When you look up the word "used," one of the words in the definition is "successful." If we know what to do in order to become successful, shouldn't we do that? Cain obviously was a little careless about the system and science of success until it really mattered; by then it was too late. If we do what we know is right and successful, we will be accepted, we will be elevated, or as the Bible says, exalted.

Just the opposite will occur if we don't work toward success and the things that are right—"sin lies at the door." "Sin" is the word *chatta'ah* (khat-taw-aw´), which means an offense. Offense is a sin toward God and toward man. Offense is a killer of God's anointing and purposes. Offense separates us from God and from people whom God may have sent to us. I don't think anything happens by accident—someone is always planning. When you and God are not planning, the enemy is. If we don't plan for success and create a plan in which God can use us, most certainly the devil will plan some form of default for your life.

He lies at the door with a trap or a snare in his hand. Waiting for you to step into the trap and at the moment you fall into his trap, he pulls the trigger of his trap and captures your heart with offense. The enemy is lurking and waiting to see if you will do what is right and successful or if you will try to get away with anything you can. He wants to see if you will take a shortcut even though you know the right way to create success. Please keep in mind that the enemy is lurking, waiting, and hoping that you will take that shortcut.

FAMILIAR SPIRITS

The devil's passion is to destroy you and your destiny, "And [sin's] desire is for you, but you should rule over it" (Gen. 4:7b). His desire is to control you, to stress you out, and to create need in your life. Once that happens, you will have to work very hard in order to get the upper hand again.

When you give in to his trap, you develop soul ties and attract familiar spirits that are bent on dragging you down. A familiar spirit is a fallen angel that is sent to you by satan and has liberty to move in certain areas of your life because of an open door of sin. Familiar spirits work against you; they work against your marriage, against your business, or any other place that God would want to bless you. The enemy will send a familiar spirit that will keep you looking for more and more shortcuts. It is like a gambler who wins a great hand at the blackjack table and eventually becomes addicted to the excitement of winning. Convinced that he has been given a run of luck, he then bets everything and loses it all. Falling into an even deeper and stronger trap, he spends the rest of the night or several nights trying to regain his losses. Familiar spirits assigned to you will create failure in your life by leading you into fleshly and unhealthy circumstances.

Spirits such as the spirit of control, the spirit of fear, and the spirit of rejection are spirits that can influence and control your life. The Bible refers to them as "familiar spirits," which are spirits usually connected to divination. Have you ever met someone who you instantly wanted to reject? Even though you don't know them, you have an immediate desire to dismiss them and you have an urge to stay away from them. Often, this is the spirit of rejection influencing you. Several times I have worked to get to know someone who I felt had a familiar spirit, only to discover that they have been experiencing rejection all their life. I have encouraged them to forgive people who have broken covenants and have helped them develop strong and unconditional relationships.

I have found that many people live without the understanding of familiar spirits and easily give in to these spirits when they come into contact with them. But God says, "Give no regard to mediums and familiar spirits; do not seek after them, to be defiled by them: I am the Lord your God" (Lev. 19:31). These familiar spirits communicated with the fortunetellers in biblical days and told them everything they wanted to know about the person whom they were familiar with. They would follow that person journalizing and taking notes of that person and their family. Current-day psychics interact with familiar spirits, whereas Christians know the past, present, and future through the help of the Holy Spirit. Familiar spirits know your weaknesses and play off them. You must first overcome these evils in order to establish healthy covenants, otherwise they will destroy covenants in your life.

SELFISH AMBITION

Now Cain talked with Abel his brother; and it came to pass, when they were in the field, that Cain rose up against Abel his brother and killed him. Then the Lord said to Cain, "Where

*is Abel your brother?" He said, "I do not know. Am I my
brother's keeper?"* (Genesis 4:8-9)

Cain's offense led him to kill his brother. When God confronted Cain about the disappearance of his brother, Cain's response revealed his heart, "Am I my brother's keeper?" Am I my
brother's guard? Am I my brother's protector? Am I my brother's covenant partner? If these two brothers would have been
each other's guard and covenant partner, Cain would have been
accepted and Abel would have never been murdered.

Cain created much more trouble than he realized. He
caused grief for his parents, for God, and for his community.

*And He said, "What have you done? The voice of your broth-
er's blood cries out to Me from the ground. So now you are
cursed from the earth, which has opened its mouth to receive
your brother's blood from your hand. When you till the ground,
it shall no longer yield its strength to you. A fugitive and a
vagabond you shall be on the earth."* (Genesis 4:10-12).

The ground called out to God for vengeance. The earth
cursed Cain because Cain had polluted it. I believe when land
cries out against spilled blood, it will not be able to yield fruit.
This is what most of our cities are suffering from—the polluted
ground refusing to yield its best. Polluted ground is sick ground.
There is a video called "Transformations" produced by The Sentinel Group, which shows polluted ground restored through
corporate prayer and repentance. After repentance and prayer,
the ground began to yield fruit—not just any fruit, but produce
of extravagant size—a significant change in criminal activity and
citywide prosperity. Many places in the world have experienced
great breakthroughs because of repentance and prayer.

The ground cried out against Cain because Abel's murder
involved the shedding and spilling of blood for selfish reasons.
All bloodshed before this day had been for the sake of getting
closer to God, whereas Abel's blood was spilled in vain. There

was no purpose for his spilled blood. Bloodshed was to be reserved for establishing covenant. Cain neglected to establish a covenant with God because he didn't bring blood to God, and he did not establish a covenant with his brother because he did not guard him. Instead, he murdered him. Jesus said that, "You shall love the Lord your God with all your heart, with all your soul, with all your strength, and with all your mind, and your neighbor as yourself" (Lk. 10:27). Cain failed on all accounts. God has set before us life and death. In order for you to choose life, you must reject things that cause death. Because Cain chose not to establish a covenant with God or man, he couldn't receive favor from God or man. Not making covenants or not keeping covenants are choices that eventually lead to death. Let's consider a few covenant breakers and death choices. These are sins of the soul.

THE PITFALL OF LUST

When the children of Israel departed from Egypt, it wasn't long before they desired things that were not good for them—they wanted to go back to Egypt, they wanted a golden calf, and they wanted different food than God was providing. Eventually, God gave them many of their desires, but not without a price. Psalm 106:15 says, "And He gave them their request, but sent leanness into their soul."

There was a price for their lust—a lust for things that God didn't plan for them to have. The consequence for receiving and giving in to lust is leanness or thinness in your soul. Leanness in the soul creates weakness in your emotions, weakness in thoughts, weakness in your intentions, and most of all, it affects your willpower. A soul with leanness no longer has the power to say no to wrong things or resist the animal nature of man. We must avoid lust in order to protect our souls.

Where do wars and fights come from among you? Do they not come from your desires for pleasure that war in your members?

You lust and do not have. You murder and covet and cannot obtain. You fight and war. Yet you do not have because you do not ask. You ask and do not receive, because you ask amiss, that you may spend it on your pleasures (James 4:1-3).

Lust is self-seeking, yet lust doesn't guarantee that you will get what you desire. The Scripture above actually confirms the idea that lust produces nothing but war and trouble. Love never lacks, while lust always fails. "Let us love one another, for love is of God" (1 Jn. 4:7a).

THE PITFALL OF PRIDE

Lust is very dangerous, yet pride is even more dangerous. A prideful heart doesn't acknowledge that there is anything wrong within. A proud person never even notices when he is lusting; he continues to believe that he is on track with God and full of godliness. The sin of pride can be broken, only by humility. The Bible says, "God resists the proud, but gives grace to the humble" (Jas. 4:6b).

Often pride comes after success. Many great people have lost everything they have worked for because of pride. Sometimes pride hinders success. Either way, pride leads to shame, strife, and destruction.

When pride comes, then comes shame; but with the humble is wisdom (Proverbs 11:2).

By pride comes nothing but strife, but with the well-advised is wisdom (Proverbs 13:10).

Pride goes before destruction, and a haughty spirit before a fall. Better to be of a humble spirit with the lowly, than to divide the spoil with the proud (Proverbs 16:18-19).

The previous Scriptures from Proverbs remind us that pride leads to shame, strife, and destruction, but wisdom is in the heart of the humble. Wisdom is the key to everything that we desire, and the Bible says that the fear of God is the beginning of wisdom. You are safe from pride as long as you have a fear of God. However, where there is a lack of a fear of the Lord, there is also a lack of wisdom and humility, but abundance of pride.

Not all pride comes from an arrogant heart; some pride comes from a fearful heart. The pride of life is a product of fear. The pride of life will cause the things of the world to be more important than the things of God. It causes us to worry about what we have and what we do not have. First John 2:16 says, "For all that is in the world—the lust of the flesh, the lust of the eyes, and the pride of life—is not of the Father but is of the world." The pride of life is worldly and just as destructive as the pride of arrogance. It causes you to work hard for something only to find that the harder you work, the further away the goal becomes. Ultimately, the pride of life leads to jealousy and envy.

THE PITFALL OF ENVY

For where envy and self-seeking exist, confusion and every evil thing are there. But the wisdom that is from above is first pure, then peaceable, gentle, willing to yield, full of mercy and good fruits, without partiality and without hypocrisy (James 3:16-17).

Envy creates confusion.

Many times I've had to deal with someone who had envy in his or her heart. The relationship starts off great, but after a while, comments are made and attitudes are revealed. It usually catches me off guard. I become confused, and all of a sudden, the relationship starts to go sour—and in my mind, for no reason. Later, I discover that there was some form of envy in their heart. These people are usually very competitive, comparing what they have and what they are doing to what others have and are doing. When you come into contact with someone like this, mark him or her, and protect yourself.

God will give you wisdom that will help them and help you. So many times, God has warned me about envious people, and many times God has given me added wisdom by warning me not to be envious of others. I am naturally competitive, but God knows that I have a great fear of Him. This fear causes me to stand up at attention when God starts to warn me about not being envious of others. The fear of God will keep you wise; consequently, wisdom systematically adds to you purity, peace, gentleness, the ability to be taught, mercifulness, productivity, sincerity, and a life without prejudice. Those things are the fruits of wisdom. Whereas, the fruits of envy are confusion and every evil thing according to First John. Envy leads to every evil thing. Think about all the evil in the world, all the evil that takes place in Africa, in Israel, in the urban areas of the U.S. and even in our schools. All these evils have a root of envy somewhere in their genealogy. Seeking self, instead of seeking the Kingdom of God, leads to confusion and all the evils in the world.

Why should we waste our lives seeking something for ourselves when God is already looking out for our best benefit? Abraham wrote a covenant with God, which is a part of our inheritance. If we keep this covenant with God, God will keep the covenant with us. What is our duty in keeping the covenant? We must live for God. We must build His Kingdom. We must protect His interest. And when we seek His best interest, He will keep His covenant. God promised Abraham that he and his descendants would be blessed and multiply.

> *Delight yourself also in the Lord, and He shall give you the desires of your heart. Commit your way to the Lord, trust also in Him, and He shall bring it to pass* (Psalm 37:4-5).

God keeps His covenant by ordering our steps. God-ordered steps always lead to the desires of our heart.

LUCIFER'S DOWNFALL

Lucifer had it made. As part of God's team, he was guaranteed success as long as he stayed with God. In the Scripture, however, we learn that lucifer wanted to be exalted—not just *within* God's Kingdom, but over God's Kingdom. Today, lucifer is not happy having his own followers and his own kingdom; he wants God's Kingdom as well. He doesn't just want to be better than God; he enviously wants to replace God.

There is a small difference between jealousy and envy. I believe that jealousy and envy both desire to have what someone else has, but envy goes one step further. Envy not only desires what someone else has, but it also wants to take what the other person has away from them, and have it only for themselves.

Look at what the Scripture says about Lucifer's thought life:

For you have said in your heart: "I will ascend into heaven, I will exalt my throne above the stars of God; I will also sit on the mount of the congregation on the farthest sides of the north; I will ascend above the heights of the clouds, I will be like the Most High" (Isaiah 14:13-14).

Everything about success that lucifer learned, he learned from watching how God governed His Kingdom. However, there is one major point that lucifer continues to fail to recognize: God is the Creator! He creates from nothing and makes something. Even if lucifer could be God for a day, he would fail because he lacks the ability to create. At best, he is a master copycat.

Even now, satan's kingdom doesn't possess any creative ability. He doesn't have the ability to make something from nothing; he is not a creator. He takes what already exists and uses it. He renovates God's creation, adds his ingredients that pollute it, and sticks his name on it. He is very envious of God's relationship with us, so he tries to destroy our relationship and confidence in God. His favorite tool to convince us to break our covenant with God is to deceive us into believing his lies.

Satan can't deceive your body or spirit, but he can deceive your mind; and once it is deceived, you will then abuse your body through drugs, alcohol, sexual sins, and bad eating habits.

Satan will cause you to neglect God, His gifts, and His plan for your life.

DECEPTION

By removing these three vain emotions of lust, pride, and envy, that eventually lead to vain imaginations, we protect ourselves from the devices of the enemy. We cannot afford to be ignorant of his devices. If we are, he will surely take advantage of us.

> *Lest Satan should take advantage of us; for we are not ignorant of his devices* (2 Corinthians 2:11).

In order to avoid ignorance, you must learn to discern what is right and what is wrong. You must learn to discern every voice, every opportunity, and every person and examine them according to the Word of God and the example of Christ. The first check is: Is it biblical? Do you see its pattern in the Bible? The second check. Is it Christ like? Thirdly: Is it benefiting and building the Kingdom of God? Finally, does it represent the fruit of the Spirit? The fruits of the Spirit are my ultimate source for discernment. Even though I frequently receive prophetic words, words of knowledge, and words of wisdom, I cannot rely on my interpretation of these gifts without the help of the Holy Spirit and His manifestation of His fruit in my life. If I don't feel peace, then I will put it aside until I get peace. If I never receive a peace about it, it will remain on the shelf forever. We never have to run in haste when we are trusting in God. Isaiah 52:12 says, "For you shall not go out with haste, nor go by flight; for the Lord will go before you, and the God of Israel will be your rear guard." Always check your inner witness. The fruit of the Spirit will never misguide you nor can you be deceived when you learn to be led by the fruit of the Spirit.

Again, always get a second opinion, even if an angel has come to you, or a prophet has prophesied, or you have heard a still small voice. Always get confirmation. God is big enough and good enough to make sure that you receive confirmation. This simple checklist is a sure way to keep from being deceived by the enemy. If every voice, opportunity, and person who you desire to embrace makes it through this checklist, you will find success at the end of the journey. Every creative thought and every imagination should be tested through this checklist. God speaks to us through our imagination but so does the enemy. Yet we can easily expose his devices and defuse his lies, so that we can clearly receive insight and understanding from God through our imagination.

The enemy wants your heart for his desires. He wants to live through you. If he can make you lose heart, he will overcome you and cause you to walk separate from God and His plan for your life. Consequently, God must then reject you. But to our great benefit, God searches our heart to make sure that we are like Him. King David taught this to Solomon in First Chronicles 28:9, saying:

> *And thou, Solomon my son, know thou the God of thy father, and serve Him with a perfect heart and with a willing mind: for the Lord searcheth all hearts, and understandeth all the imaginations of the thoughts: if thou seek Him, He will be found of thee; but if thou forsake Him, He will cast thee off for ever* (1 Chronicles 28:9).

We must stay loyal to God and to the Kingdom of God; our loyalty will then keep us from being flattered by the enemy and worldliness. Our loyalty ensures that we remain teachable and submitted to God. God is not difficult to find—you need only to set your heart to seek Him and He will make Himself known to you. If we know God, we cannot be distracted or deceived by the enemy. Knowing God keeps us strong as we do great things for Him.

To Be or Not to Be...Bitter

Another cunning and crafty device of the enemy is strife. Through strife, the enemy not only wants to cause division; he also wants us to become bitter. Bitterness destroys everything that it touches. When you develop a bitter heart, satan begins to destroy you and anyone who comes in contact with you. Bitterness hardens your heart, rots your bones, and pushes people away.

Strife does lead to bitterness, but that doesn't mean we have to give in to strife. If you understand where strife comes from, then you can see beyond the strife and study the bigger picture. One of the things I learned is that if you don't give in to the enemy's game, God can bless you and make sure you receive everything that belongs to you.

Isaac learned to make the best of every opportunity; we see that from the beginning. When he became prosperous, Abimelech told him to go away because he was growing in might, so mighty that Isaac became a threat. And here, Isaac's journey and battle with strife begins. When we threaten the enemy by pursuing the best that God has for us, he will start working on a plan to destroy God's purpose for us.

Issac willingly left town and ended up in Gerar. *Gerar* means a temporary lodging place. It was not Isaac's destiny nor was it where Isaac wanted to be. Even so, while in Gerar, Isaac attempted to re-dig and restore one of the wells that his father Abraham had dug, because it had been filled with dirt and stopped up by the Philistines. When the herdsmen of Gerar came and fought him for the well, Isaac named the well *Essek*, which means "strife." Any time you attempt to accomplish something great, the first thing the enemy will do is cause strife. Strife will get your eyes off the goal and onto the people you are striving with. The first strife you will encounter is contention. This contention is what I call level-one strife; it consists of words and attitudes, criticism, and snide remarks. It comes from those people who should be your allies.

Later, Isaac re-dug another one of his father's wells, and again there was quarreling. Isaac named this well *Sitnah*, which means "enmity, a deep hatred, and hostility." What starts as a little contention can turn into hatred and hostility. Hostility describes a strife that works against you, either through oppression or force. If the enemy can't convince you to stop your pursuit through strife, he will try to stop you by force and hostility.

After this fight, Isaac moved on; he felt that the territory was not worth fighting for. He traveled to another area and dug another well—not one of his father's wells, but his own well. He named this well *Rehoboth*, which means, "God has opened a wide-open place for me." Here is where the lesson started for me.

The first thing I noticed was that strife occurred in a temporary place. Gerar was a temporary lodging place. It was not Isaac's destined place; it was simply a place on the way to his destiny. It was his proving ground and his testing place. You will encounter strife on the way to your promised land, but never in your promised land. Sometimes your circumstances and surroundings will be totally peaceful on your way to the promised land, and suddenly out of nowhere, strife will pounce upon you. It can come at you from people you love or from people who have little to do with you. Most often, strife comes from people whom God is moving out of your way, who would be a hindrance in the future to your purpose. Don't fret when people are suddenly removed out of your life, so suddenly that it seems supernatural—that's because it is God, and when it's God, it's good. It can be the best thing that you have ever experienced. It will save you years of heartache. If they are to be covenant partners with you, God will bring about another opportunity for the covenant to be established. If you are currently experiencing strife, know first that it is temporary and secondly...it is temporary. You are now moving through the testing ground. Once Isaac made it to

Rehoboth, the strife stopped. How you handle this time is more important than where you are located.

The next lesson I learned was sometimes it is more godly to walk away from strife than to fight it out. When I first read this story, I wanted Isaac to stand up for himself. I thought, *What a wimp*, when he walked away instead of standing up to them and fighting. But the opposite is true. What an awesome man of God he was; in walking away, he probably kept his heart from bitterness. Isaac had a right to fight for his inheritance. These wells were dug by his father and rightly belonged to him, but they were not his promised land. Why get caught up with things that don't help your vision and your purpose? I always ask myself, "Will it matter in five years? Will I feel the same about it then, as I do today?" Most of the time the answer is no. But if I give in to the strife, I will still be experiencing the same feelings five years from now, because bitterness never forgets nor forgives. It will be just as fresh in your heart and memory then as it was on the first day you bore the grief.

Isaac didn't get caught up with the temporary nor did he suffer from bitterness. For those reasons, God visited him. Not only did God visit him, but God also confirmed the covenant that Abraham his father made with Him and with Abimelech. Isaac gained favor with God and with man.

> *And the Lord appeared to him the same night and said, "I am the God of your father Abraham; do not fear, for I am with you. I will bless you and multiply your descendants for My servant Abraham's sake." So he built an altar there and called on the name of the Lord, and he pitched his tent there; and there Isaac's servants dug a well. Then Abimelech came to him from Gerar with Ahuzzath, one of his friends, and Phichol the commander of his army. And Isaac said to them, "Why have you come to me, since you hate me and have sent me away from you?" But they said, "We have certainly seen that the Lord is with you. So we said, 'Let there now be an*

oath between us, between you and us; and let us make a
covenant with you, that you will do us no harm, since we
have not touched you, and since we have done nothing to you
but good and have sent you away in peace. You are now the
blessed of the Lord' " (Genesis 26:24-29).

Overcome strife by pursuing peace and the purposes of
God, and God will give you favor with God and with man. If we
choose not to take matters into our own hands, God will fight
for us. This is a New Testament revelation, which is exemplified
in the Old Testament.

Therefore "If your enemy is hungry, feed him; if he is thirsty,
give him a drink; for in so doing you will heap coals of fire on
his head." Do not be overcome by evil, but overcome evil with
good (Romans 12:20-21).

Isaac heaped hot coals on his enemy's head and God
showed him favor. I know our nature wants revenge, but God
wants righteousness. There will ultimately be revenge, but first
we must do it God's way. We must purge our soul from all pollu-
tion of the enemy and from anything that is contrary to the
Kingdom of God.

PURGING THE SOUL

You don't need to stand in a deliverance line in order to receive deliverance. The Collins Minigem English Dictionary defines *deliver* as "carry to destination" or "release." God wants us
to be free from everything that would hinder our destiny. So
when God delivers us, He carries us to our destination, allowing
us to see the end before we actually possess it. I believe that you
must have a clear-cut view of your destination in order to truly
be free and stay free. God wants you to see the future so vividly
that you are willing to let go of anything that is mediocre and resist any temptation of the enemy.

This kind of deliverance can happen in your car, in your kitchen, or in a church. There is no one specific place where God cannot reach someone who will dream and envision themselves living in and wallowing in freedom. But...you will never possess what you do not first see.

Again, we must go back to the soul and its health. If your future success, prosperity, and health are determined by the health of your soul, then you must have a soul free from soul ties and leanness. Soul ties are emotional chains that bind you to certain thinking, emotional dependence, or bondage. Soul ties fasten you to something or someone who holds your attention and has a stronger grip on you than the dream and visions of God have on you. Leanness in the soul are fault lines that move and fracture under pressure. You have no stability in your life; the smallest things cause you to quake and shake. You cannot commit or stay faithful to things that you have promised to do. You may have a desire to do things right, but you lack the willpower to fulfill that desire. These things have to be overcome before you can experience the blessings of a healthy soul.

The Holy Spirit communicates through your soul, the doorway into the Spirit. When I first was saved, I received some incredible instructions from God that helped me work through the soul ties and leanness that I encumbered in the world. One day as I was praying in my room, I suddenly saw in my imagination a door. Whether it was a vision or imagery, I don't think it matters because I have used this revelation many times since, and have experienced great freedom from weakness in my soul. Over the doorpost of this door I saw a word; the word was "anger." I then saw Jesus opening the door and commanding a spirit out of that door. After the spirit of anger left through that door, Jesus closed the door and covered the doorpost with His blood. On that day I was released from the spirit of anger, and I knew that the only way anger would control my life again would be the day that I chose to open my heart's door again to the spirit of anger. I know that this sounds a little unconventional; but do deliverance or healing lines seem any more conventional? Week after week, the Holy Spirit would show me something else I needed to release. I would go into my room and pray, and while praying I would imagine Jesus going to the door, opening the door, commanding the weakness to leave, closing the door, and covering the doorpost with His blood. Fear, unbelief, lust, jealousy, selfishness, or whatever you may be dealing with, can be purged from your soul and heart through this kind of deliverance. The Bible calls it renewing your mind. While you reformat your mind to the right thoughts and character, the Holy Spirit works with you, and the authority of Jesus sets you free from all leanness and soul ties. Just as the destroyer had to pass over the children of Israel's homes because of the blood on their doorposts, he will also pass over the blood on your door.

> And you shall take a bunch of hyssop, dip it in the blood that is in the basin, and strike the lintel and the two doorposts with the blood that is in the basin. And none of you shall go out of the door of his house until morning. For the Lord will pass through to strike the Egyptians; and when He sees the blood on the lintel and on the two doorposts, the Lord will pass over the door and not allow the destroyer to come into your houses to strike you (Exodus 12:22-23).

Leanne Payne writes in her book, *The Healing Presence*:

No one can "heal" anyone of bad mental or moral habits. Such a one is responsible for confessing these and then for "taking them off" and for "putting on the new." Our prayers for that person must be dramatically and graphically toward that end, and it will be, in effect, the work of baptism. The imagery is incarnational. It has to do with taking one's place in Christ and of Christ's resurrection life in us. But this is something the one who comes for healing does, not us, and we will always see God do His part once they've made the decision to put off their sin and slothfulness.[2]

Healing and deliverance must take place in your soul before they can take place in your body and in your life.

It is very important that we take responsibility for the things we have encumbered ourselves with and not to blame anyone else for our weaknesses and flaws. Until we own up to the fact that we have caused chaos in our own lives, we will not deal with those sins properly. Instead of repenting and allowing Jesus to set us free, we will tend to blame others for our faults—blaming others will never cause freedom. We must allow the blood of Jesus to cover the door of our soul and imagine freedom from those things that easily beset us.

Once I received freedom in my soul from things that were hindering my growth, I then had to learn to keep my freedom. I needed to learn to fight using the Jesus style of fighting—contend.

CONTENTION AND SPIRITUAL WARFARE

In the Book of Jude, we are encouraged to contend for the faith that was once and for all delivered to the saints. "Beloved, while I was very diligent to write to you concerning our common salvation, I found it necessary to write to you exhorting you to contend earnestly for the faith which was once for all delivered to the saints" (Jude 1:3).

We must contend for confidence that the enemy wants to steal. We are not to contend just for the sake of contending, but we must contend for the faith. We all can have the same faith that Paul the apostle had if we are willing to contend for it.

The first Greek word that formulates "contend" is *epi* (ep-ee´), meaning "superimposition"—in other words, to place a façade over it or to put something over it. The enemy wants to project over you what he believes, whether that is sickness, poverty, hatred, or jealousy. He wants to steal your confidence through superimposing his vision for your life over the intention of God. In order to contend, you must refuse what the enemy is saying and replace it with what God is saying. If he says, "You are a failure," you must replace his thoughts with God's thoughts; you must respond to him, "I am more than a conqueror!" The second word is *agonizomai* (ag-o-nid´-zom-ahee), which means, "to struggle." Struggle with the lying tongue of the enemy until you overcome what he has been saying and you gain full and complete confidence in what God will do in your life. Struggling is not saying, "Get out of my life" only one time and then accepting what comes next. Struggling is a stubbornness that refuses to have anything except what God has determined for you. Keep the faith, by keeping your confidence. Contention is of God as long as it is in the spirit realm and is accomplished for God's perfect will. Our contentions are soulish and spiritual. Our warfare is soulish and spiritual. We must fight the enemy in our soul and in the spirit.

> *For though we walk in the flesh, we do not war according to the flesh. For the weapons of our warfare are not carnal but mighty in God for pulling down strongholds, casting down arguments and every high thing that exalts itself against the knowledge of God, bringing every thought into captivity to the obedience of Christ* (2 Corinthians 10:3-5).

We must win the battle in our soul before we can win the battle in the spirit. We must "pull down strongholds." Strongholds are mental caves and isolated thinking patterns that prevent us from moving forward and having success. We must use our mighty weapons in order to ensure victory. God's weapon of warfare is His Word—the written Word and the spoken word. We can use the surer word of prophecy, a creative thought, and the spoken word of God to combat strongholds. Some strongholds are devil-inspired, some are man-inspired through false teaching, some are traditions of men, and some are formed from unbelief. But no matter where the strongholds come from, they need to be pulled down.

Why must they come down? Why can't they be broken instead? They must be pulled down because strongholds are thoughts that have been exalted above the knowledge of God. That means that they have been exalted above God's Word, God's name, the truth, and anything else that represents godliness and goodness. And we must use the Word to bring them down. The Word of God is the highest form of authority. God has exalted His Word even above His name (see Ps. 138:2). If we use the Word and cause every one of the devil's thoughts and every vain imagination to be subjected to the Word of God, we will have ultimate favor and ultimate victory.

These thoughts must be imprisoned by the Word or by the obedience of Christ. Christ is the Word, so we must obey Christ. A better way of saying this is to say that we must obey the way that Christ obeyed. Obedience is our weapon. Simply quoting the Word is not an effective form of spiritual and soulish warfare alone; you must also have obedience of the Word in your heart in order for you to have credence in the Kingdom of God. Your obedience captures the lies of the enemy and takes away any form of condemnation and accusation. Most of the time, the enemy accuses us of things that we are truly guilty of, but Jesus has set us free.

And being ready to punish all disobedience when your obedience is fulfilled (2 Corinthians 10:6).

In order to obey, we must be ready. We must be flexible, adjustable, pliable. If God wants to change something in us, all He has to do is show us. We must take the offensive stance; we need not defend. The Strong's Dictionary gives us such a wonderful description of the word *punish*. It's *ekdikeo* (ek-dik-eh´-o)—to vindicate, retaliate, punish. You see, God is not against us retaliating in the spirit realm. It is only in the natural realm that God wants to fight for us. We must allow God to keep His end of the covenant. We are weak in the natural so He fights for us while we serve as His bondservants. We have been given mighty weapons of warfare from God's arsenal so that we can join Him in the spiritual fight.

What should we be taking revenge on? On disobedience. What does that mean? Disobedience is the word *parakoe* (par-ak-o-ay´), which means "inattention." This means not paying attention, choosing not to hear. The Word of God is the higher power and the highest authority and whoever chooses not to hear the Word and obey it must be arrested by the Word. A disobedient person is not a person who doesn't know any better; a disobedient person *chooses* not to hear and obey. Ignorance is having no knowledge. Disobedience is when a person knows to do better and refuses to do so.

The next words in the verse are very important—"when your obedience is fulfilled." What?! Our punishing ability is based upon our completion of obedience. Can you guess what *obedience* means in the Greek? Yes, just the opposite of disobedience; it's the word *hupakoe* (hoop-ak-o-ay´), meaning "attentive hearkening, compliance, or submission." Attentive hearing, listening with your whole heart, is fulfilling what you have been directed to do. That's the greatest form of spiritual warfare. Hearing and obeying the voice of God, the Word of God, or the creative thoughts of God are more devastating to the kingdom of darkness. Any other form of spirit warfare must be founded in obedience; otherwise, it is not spiritual warfare at all. When we declare the Word, when we worship, when we intercede, when we give—all these forms of warfare must be rooted in obedience.

Jesus overcame the enemy in the wilderness by obedience. He used the Word until He heard the voice of God, at which time He used the spoken word and overcame the enemy. When Jesus heard God say, "He shall not tempt the Lord your God," Jesus rebuked the devil saying, "It has been said, 'You shall not tempt the Lord your God' " (Lk. 4:12b). From this encounter, Jesus received power and the devil fled in weakness. The punishment of disobedience starts at the completion of your obedience. If you set a standard of obedience, God will trust you with authority prescriptions and creative thoughts.

ENDNOTES

1. Casey Treat, *Renewing the Mind* (Tulsa, OK: Harrison House, 1992), 82.

2. Leanne Payne, *The Healing Presence* (Grand Rapids, MI: Baker Books, 1989).

~ CHAPTER SIX ~

CREATIVE THOUGHT

*By faith we understand that the universe was formed at God's
command, so that what is seen was not made out of what was
visible* (Hebrews 11:3 NIV).

CREATIVITY EQUALS FAITH

God creates what doesn't exist. He doesn't create from
things that are already available. He is not limited to what He
sees in the natural. God starts with a void and forms something
from nothing.

Creativity is not modifying what already is. Creativity is seeing what does not exist without any prior reference point or
knowledge. Inventors are creative people who tap into the mysteries and secrets of the universe allowing them to imagine
things that only God Himself has thought of. Creative thoughts
are God's thoughts alone.

The Bible calls this faith. Faith is more than believing;
faith must involve the ability to see things that can't be seen. If

a person has belief alone, he will never possess ample desire and conviction to create; his belief will become mere hope or even fear. Many Christians try to achieve their heart's desire in the name of faith, rehearsing and convincing themselves that what they desire is their right, only to be disappointed. It is spiritual sight that produces an intestinal fortitude, an absolute confidence that cannot be denied. If you have only the rehearsing of hopes and dreams without conviction, you are wasting your time. This kind of mental and emotional activity moves your hope further and further away from fruition, causing you to feel sick and depressed about your future. A sick heart is a by-product of a fearful heart and will eventually cause utter disappointment. Repetition in and of itself cannot be faith unless a creative thought, not mere assumptions, inspires the repetition.

Without creative thoughts, you will never be able to see your future clearly enough to take steps toward it. Real faith is the intricately clear creative thought that is produced by desire, and the confidence of it coming to pass by means greater than you. Hebrews 11:1 says, "Now faith is the substance of things hoped for, the evidence of things not seen."

We must be able to describe without insecurity and hesitation what we are looking for. If I went to a restaurant and said to the waiter, "Please bring me a plate of *food*," the waiter would give me a menu and reply, "Take a look at the menu so that you can choose exactly what you want." I may respond, "Just bring me anything. I just want something to eat—I am hungry!" Hungry I may be, but until I can describe what I want, the waiter cannot deliver my desire. The same is true with faith. You must be able to give a distinct description of what you are hoping for. Dr. Paul Yonggi Cho in *The Fourth Dimension* writes about how his prayer life changed after receiving a specific type of desk, chair, and bicycle that he had requested. "Until that time I had always prayed in vague terms, but from that time until now I have never prayed in vague terms. If God were ever to answer your vague prayers, then you would never recognize that prayer as being answered by God. You must ask definitely and specifically."[1]

The Lord never welcomes vague prayers. When the son of Timaeus, blind Bartimaeus, heard that Jesus was passing by, he cried, "Jesus, Son of David, have mercy on me!" (Mk. 10:47b) Although everyone knew that Bartimaeus was asking for healing of his blindness, Christ asked, "What do you want Me to do for You?" Christ wants us to ask specifically. Bartimaeus answered, "Rabboni, that I may receive my sight" (Mk. 10:51b). Jesus replied, "Go your way; your faith has made you well" (Mk. 10:52a). And Bartimaeus opened his eyes.

When you bring your request to the Lord, come with a specific request, a definite objective, and a clear-cut goal. Faith can never remain general; faith demands that your mind and heart graphically visualize the end result before you have it.

VISION FOR THE FUTURE

When I was hoping for a new car, I could see exactly what kind and color of car I wanted. When it came to acquiring my heart's desire, I was able to describe specifically what I wanted. And today, I have that car in my garage. Maybe the make and model of your car is not important to you, but you should have a clear picture of what you want for your marriage, for your children, for your business, and for your future.

You can possess anything in your future by what you describe with conviction and confidence today. You must be able to see into the mind of God's imagination in order to receive vivid creative thought that will enable you to have faith. Faith is nothing without seeing and acting upon what you see, and seeing is ineffective without God's imagination. James makes it clear to us that faith is truly action: "For as the body without the spirit is dead, so faith without works is dead also" (Jas. 2:26).

Jesus was walking with His disciples one day, when He, finding Himself hungry, noticed a fig tree. He had hoped to find some figs to eat, but when He found none on the tree, He spoke to the fruitless tree, "Let no fruit grow on you ever again" (Mt. 21:19b); and the tree immediately withered away. The disciples were amazed by the affect of Jesus' words. Jesus replied to His disciples, "Assuredly, I say to you, if you have faith and do not doubt, you will not only do what was done to the fig tree, but also if you say to this mountain, 'Be removed and be cast into the sea,' it will be done" (Mt. 21:21). Jesus' hunger had created a desire for Him to eat a fig from that tree. However, at that time, the tree had no way of fulfilling His need as He spoke to it. I believe this experience showed His disciples that He had the power to remove from His life anything that was barren or hindering. He then turned to His disciples and said if they spoke by the creative imagination of God, they too could overcome any obstacle or hindrance in their lives.

Your ability to see, directly affects your ability to understand. Let's go back to the story about Zerubbabel. After the angel said to Zerubbabel, "Not by might nor by power, but by My Spirit, says the Lord of hosts" (Zech. 4:6), he continued by speaking to the mountain that stood before Zerubbabel, saying, "Who are you, O great mountain? Before Zerubbabel you shall become a plain! And he shall bring forth the capstone with shouts of 'Grace, grace to it!' " Once Zerubbabel saw and understood the creative thought, he was given the power to overcome his mountain. The mountain was no longer an issue. His words were now words of authority. By shouting, "Grace, grace," he could stop the intimidation and the humiliation of his limitations by understanding that creative thoughts release the grace of God to accomplish what is seen.

Need—The Womb of Invention

Needs can seem like mountains, but I believe you must first have a need before you can develop creativity. Need is the womb of invention. Every invention has been created as a result of a need. Let's think about this. Without a need, there is really no reason for change. So, in order to progress, we must first recognize our limitation. Limitation causes dissatisfaction, which in turn should cause us to seek a different way of doing things, or discover what we are missing. Our need should cause a greater and clearer vision of what we want. A clear vision mixed with a positive God-image will produce a supernatural ability to first, *think* outside the box and second, *walk* outside the box. The process is very clear. Need produces hope, hope gives sight, sight becomes the emotion of desire, and desire causes us to speak of what we see, stimulating us to walk toward the end result.

If we speak the creative thought that we see, we will be motivated to step into the invention. Miraculous power is produced by the God-induced imagination once someone is confronted with a need. Inventors create new inventions from this sphere of the invisible. Remember, inventions are the answers to problems, the solution to an everyday need in your life. In the book, *The Marketing Imagination,* by Theodore Levitt, he writes, "By asserting that people don't buy things but buy solutions to problems, the marketing imagination makes an inspired leap from the obvious to the meaningful. 'Meaning' resides in its implied suggestion as to what to do—in this case, find out what problems people are trying to solve."[2] Financial success comes from the ability to imagine a way to solve someone else's problems.

Most small business owners think their businesses will grow and become successful because they provide the best quality product. Having a good product is extremely important, but it is not the reason most people gain success. Other people have started businesses because they are good and talented at what they do, but they never really experience success. Why? Because they have not tapped into the God-given imagery that will help them use their talents to solve somebody's problems. Successful businessmen and women are innovators who solve problems. God allows us to have a need in order to give us inventive or creative thought. And so, your need is not only a problem, but becomes an opportunity to change the world.

PROBLEM SOLVING

Resist him, steadfast in the faith, knowing that the same sufferings are experienced by your brotherhood in the world (1 Peter 5:9).

I once heard a story of a man who desired a particular food to eat, yet he was unable to find this product in any of the stores in his community. One day while eating, he thought, *Why don't I open a store that sells specific ethnic food?* So he approached some investors about his new project, but each one turned him down. Nevertheless he remained convicted with this desire and came up with the initial investment himself. Needless to say, the store succeeded, so much so that he has now opened several other stores in his city.

It just happened that in his city, there were enough people who had the same need, craving the same food, yet none of them had a strong enough desire to move on their need. Many of us have needs that we never attempt to meet; we simply accept or tolerate them. We may find it too much work or too much bother to pursue a solution, or insecurity creeps in and steals all desire. I challenge you to look at your need as an opportunity for success, rather than seeing it as a limitation. Who knows what you shall accomplish!

Have you ever had a creative thought, an idea of some type of invention that would make your life easier, yet you never did anything about it? Then while watching late-night television two years later, you see an infomercial marketing your invention. That always drives me crazy. I have made up my mind that I will not allow that to happen again. A pastor I know says, "Somebody's going to do it—it might as well be me!" Your need doesn't have to be negative; consider it to be the best thing that has ever happened to you. When your need causes you to get a creative thought, you have just received another option. Some inventors call this, turning a problem around, or finding a problem that fits your solution!

Again, creative thoughts are thoughts that come from the imagination of God. God sees your need and He cares about your situation. It is for this very reason that God has made provision for you to overcome your need and any other limitation through Jesus. Many people want God to simply swoop down and deliver them from their problems. But God is more interested in giving us creative and inventive thoughts that will not only deliver us, but also deliver others in the world who are experiencing the same need. God's ability and creativity are limitless. This is not to say that God doesn't work miracles or that He will not spontaneously deliver us from evil. However, most miracles follow simple instructions obeyed. God wants us free, and He desires for us to stay free. So if He can show us a way out, then we can stay free with His help.

If you are in debt and I pay all your debts without teaching you how to never fall back into debt, you would continue to follow the same pattern of getting into debt over and over again. Creative thoughts not only provide a way out or a solution, but they also give you a vision to stay free. Once God gives you a creative thought, He works with you until that thought is accomplished. The Spirit of God is waiting to help you bring to pass the creative thought. The thought shows you the end result of what your life, your profession, or your situation will look like once your miracle comes to pass. It reveals to you what God is forming in you and what He desires. Creative thoughts are more than imagination; these thoughts are spiritual insights and godly intuition initiated by God.

INVENTIONS ARE SOLUTIONS

God has already spoken every invention—God has already created every profession—there is nothing new under the sun.

Creative thoughts allow us to see what God has already spoken, and they become the gates through which inventions are brought into existence. The automobile has always been created in God's mind; the paper clip was already in God's mind; God has always known of the television. Yet it took someone who would think outside the box, outside the present state, to discover these new and inventive ideas. We cannot rely on our thoughts and abilities when God can do exceedingly abundantly above all that we ask or think according to the miraculous power inside of us (see Eph. 3:20). This power is activated only when we see beyond our need. A creative thought causes you to see beyond your immediate situation.

Chester Greenwood, a 15-year-old grammar school dropout who was born in Farmington, Maine in 1858, invented earmuffs. One day while ice-skating he grew frustrated at trying to protect his ears from the cold weather. After wrapping his head in a scarf, which was too bulky and itchy, he made two ear-shaped loops from wire and asked his grandmother to sew fur on them. This invention soon gained popularity. He patented an improved model with a steel band, which held them in place, and with Greenwood's Champion Ear Protectors, he established Greenwood's Ear Protector Factory. He made a fortune supplying ear protectors to U.S. soldiers during World War I, and went on to patent more than ten other inventions.

I am sure there were thousands of people in Maine in 1858 who had cold ears, but it was a teenager who had enough initiative to do something about it. I am certain that the bitter cold stole Mr. Greenwood's happiness and joy of ice-skating, but instead of complaining and remaining in an uncomfortable state, he did something to change his circumstances. Naturally, Mr. Greenwood could not change the weather pattern, which left him with a few other options. The first was to discontinue ice-skating. That wouldn't do because he had just acquired brand new ice skates at the time. Next, he could have bore the cold.

But Mr. Greenwood desired both the freedom to skate and the comfort of warmth on his ears. So the only option left was to find comfort and protection for his ears. Young Greenwood turned his problem into profit by looking for another option instead of the obvious. His one-time problem, once solved, brought great joy, happiness, and comfort to himself and to countless of thousands in the end.

You cannot be happy in the future or the past; happiness exists only in the present. Creative thoughts from God will help you possess present joy in any set of circumstances. No matter how great your need is today, understand that God is able and willing to bring your need to an end according to His overflowing treasury. Your present lack can work for the good of many others.

One day, my wife Nathalie was warning my son not to play with an expensive vase because if he broke it, he would have to pay for it. She then asked him if he had money to pay for it. He answered, "No, but Papa does in his pocket." That is how we should approach our need—"I don't have the supply, but my Papa does." The treasure chest of God is abundant and full of possibility. Our need is nothing when we compare to it His supply that is available to us. God is just waiting for the opportunity to contribute to our needs.

Slavery is a very painful state of life for any human being, yet a man can still exercise freethinking even when he has lost his physical freedom. Thomas Jennings, a prime example, entered into a life of physical pain, yet lived in mental freedom. Thomas was born in 1791 as a slave. At the age of 30, he was the first African-American, on March 3, 1821, to receive a patent, which was for a dry-cleaning process called "dry scouring." He spent his first earnings to liberate his family from slavery and went on to be a free tradesman, operating a dry cleaning business in New York City. But his creative and inventive thought didn't stop there—he later became the assistant secretary for the First Annual Convention of People of Color in Philadelphia, Pennsylvania.

Another incredible story of greatness birthed in pain is the life of George Washington Carver. It was George Washington Carver who said, "It is not the style of clothes one wears, neither the kind of automobile one drives, nor the amount of money one has in the bank, that counts. These mean nothing. It is simply service that measures success."[3]

This seemed to be his constant life message and motto. At one time, Carver declined an invitation to work for a salary of more than $100,000 a year (the equivalent of one million dollars today). He chose instead to continue his research on behalf of his countrymen. Carver did not patent most of his products or profit from them; he freely gave his discoveries to mankind. He would say about his ideas, "God gave them to me. How can I sell them to someone else?" He went on to donate his life savings to open the Carver Research Foundation at Tuskegee.

George Washington Carver was born in 1864, in Missouri, on the farm of Moses Carver during the Civil War. George and his mother were kidnapped by Confederate night-raiders. Moses Carver found and reclaimed George after the war, yet his mother was never found. The identity of Carver's father was unknown, although Carver believed his father was a slave from a neighboring farm. Moses and Susan Carver reared George and his brothers on a farm as their own children. It was on this farm that George became familiar with different types of plants and rocks.

George went on to become an agricultural chemist and invented 300 uses for peanuts and hundreds of uses for soybeans, pecans, and sweet potatoes. Numerous products we enjoy today come from his God-birthed ideas. Among these are adhesives, cosmetics, axle grease, bleach, buttermilk, chili sauce, fuel briquettes, ink, instant coffee, linoleum, mayonnaise, meat tenderizer, metal polish, paper, plastic, pavement, shaving cream, shoe polish, synthetic rubber, talcum powder, and wood stain. He was extremely instrumental in improving the South by educating farmers to the fact that they could create more profits by developing multi-crop farmlands than by remaining a one-crop land of cotton.

George Washington Carver is a perfect example that you can overcome your upbringing with a creative and freethinking mind. God's thoughts are higher than our thoughts; God's ways are greater than our ways.

THE SEED FALLS ON FOUR TYPES OF HEARTS

It is very important that I restate that once you receive the creative thought and it enters your mind, that thought will enlighten your outlook and replace ignorance with understanding. Creative thoughts are like a light at the end of the tunnel.

Need can be considered as the soil of creative thought, while creative thought is the seed that is planted. Invention is the by-product of both coming together. But in order to have fruitfulness from a creative thought, you must also cultivate the thought in the right mind-set and perspective. Let's look at the following Scripture:

> *"Listen! Behold, a sower went out to sow. And it happened, as he sowed, that some seed fell by the wayside; and the birds of the air came and devoured it. Some fell on stony ground, where it did not have much earth; and immediately it sprang up because it had no depth of earth. But when the sun was up it was scorched, and because it had no root it withered away. And some seed fell among thorns; and the thorns grew up and choked it, and it yielded no crop. But other seed fell on good ground and yielded a crop that sprang up, increased and produced: some thirtyfold, some sixty, and some a hundred." And He said to them, "He who has ears to hear, let him hear!"* (Mark 4:3-9)

Jesus told a story of a farmer who went out to sow seed for his harvest. The farmer scattered seed on four types of ground. Each type of soil represents a type of mind-set and heart condition.

The Heart Along the Wayside

The first seed he scattered was on the wayside; the wayside represents a lack of understanding. Actually, it's more than a lack of understanding. It is an unwillingness to change and receive new understanding. If you are unwilling to change and continue to maintain a closed mind, there is no way you will ever be able to process creative thoughts. The story says that the birds will come to eat the seed before you receive a desire to pick it up.

Personal dissatisfaction must increase significantly before this mind-set will change. Desperation will need to enter the heart before the seed will have any worth or meaning. Indifferent and careless people will not recognize the seed of creativity, and the only way to destroy indifference is by generating a burning desire for success. Remember, success means different things to different people. For Mother Theresa, success was meeting the needs of the underprivileged of the world. For someone else, success may be climbing the corporate ladder of a major corporation. Success is something that each individual must define in his own mind. In any case, no one will be able to obtain success without first acquiring a burning desire for it. But when you do achieve a burning desire for success, you will change in any way necessary to accomplish it.

A Stony Heart

The farmer then scattered seed on the stony ground. The stony ground represents a heart looking for change, but has not yet determined the harvest belongs to them. Usually, stony hearts are those who have received little or no discipline in their lives. Because they have received little or no repercussions in their early lives for disobedience, they quickly get excited about every creative thought they hear but have no endurance at all to persevere. I believe when stony hearts endure enough hardships and learn obedience, they will eventually break through their stony ground.

Stony mind-sets receive the seed of creativity, but don't spend enough time dreaming of the harvest to sustain them through the tough times of invention. They are happy and joyful when they first get a glimpse of freedom, but then they start thinking about what it will take to make it happen, instead of what it will be like to harvest the crops. They may even get started on the process to bring their desire to pass, but when they run into a few obstacles or hear a few, "That has never been done before" or even a couple of "No's," what little determination they first possessed disappears, and they quit. This happens because the stony mind-set never took real ownership of the harvest. They never realized that the harvest exists only to fulfill their need. There would never be a harvest if there was no need. The harvest already belongs to you, simply because your need creates it. If you don't own the vision, you will develop a stony mind-set, and when persecution comes, the stony mind-set will abandon the dream before you can reach the harvest. Every new thought will come under persecution. Most people won't appreciate your creative thoughts, so don't take it personally when persecution arises.

A Thorny Heart

The next soil that the farmer scattered seed on was thorny ground. While trying to pick blackberries as a young boy, I became stuck in some thorny berry bushes. I was so stuck that I could not move. Not only couldn't I move, I was also afraid to move. This is exactly what the thorny mind-set will do. The thorny mind-set will be too afraid to act on what it sees. This person would have no problem finishing the project and reaping the harvest if he could just get started. Every move is like another thorn jabbing into his skin; he is so stricken with fear that he would rather stand still than go through a little pricking and prodding in order to be free, even though freedom is usually just a few uncomfortable steps away. But the thorny mind-set would rather not move than endure discomfort.

I once heard a millionaire say, "Nothing is ever accomplished without first becoming uncomfortable." Success will never be accomplished without making yourself uncomfortable as a part of the price of success. If you want your harvest, then close your eyes and tell yourself that you can handle the pain and pull free from the blackberry bushes of life. The pride of life is both fear and the need for approval, which is what plagues the thorny mind-set. Because the thorny mind-set would rather do nothing than look stupid or be seen as odd or different, he will not reap his harvest. The thorny mind-set becomes unfruitful because it is too afraid to move on what it envisions. Because fear is so paralyzing, I will dedicate a subsequent chapter to overcoming it.

A Good Heart

Finally, the last place the farmer scattered his seed on was good ground. The good ground mind-set received the creative thought; created a burning desire for it; overcame fear; and acted upon the thought. The creative thought brought such a harvest that it produced 30 times, 60 times, and even 100 times the produce. It sprung up, increased, and produced. Springing up was a sign of success; increase was the evidence that it was going to continue; and produce was more than enough for yourself and someone else. Remember, receive the creativity, dream with desire, and move on to action.

RECEIVING CREATIVE THOUGHTS

The Creator wants to constantly be involved and interact with man. God makes His thoughts known through the intuition and inspiration of our spirit-man. Yet we recognize it within our soul, because our spirit man doesn't have the ability to reason or recognize. All reasoning happens in our soul after we receive the information from God through our spirit-man. Creative thoughts can be seen with your mind's eye or heard with your inner ear. When insight comes to you, whether by intuition, which is a spiritual hearing, or by inspiration, which is a spiritual form of seeing, they should both create a picture in the mind's eye.

For example, if I show you a picture of an elephant, do you see the word "elephant" spelled out, or do you see the image of an elephant? Of course, you see the image of an elephant. Now, if I say to you, "elephant," do you see the word "elephant," or do you see the image of an elephant? Again, of course, you see the image of an elephant.

So God speaks to man by creating images in our mind. Often we call this *imagination*. Yet when God speaks, it is more than a made-up thought; it is a divinely induced thought. The Bible says that faith or confidence comes from God-induced creative thoughts, and that creative thoughts come because God has given you an ability to receive what He is speaking.

God calls those things that do not exist, as though they did. A creative thought describes something that is yet to be invented as if it is vividly in front of us, as if it has materialized. If it has never been accomplished or if it has never been created, it doesn't mean that it is impossible; it just means that no one has yet produced what God is presently showing you. Creative thoughts bring things to mind that you have never seen or heard of before. This is what caused people to get on a ship and explore uncharted waters searching for a new world. Each time you act upon a creative thought, it is like you are sailing on the Queen Mary looking for a new world.

Each time you receive a creative thought you build within your conscious a greater image of your harvest and destiny.

When a person is born again, that person's subconscious mind becomes aware of God's communication with him. Man must reconnect with his Creator, but until he does so, he will remain spiritually dead and unable to genuinely understand spiritual things. Until man makes this connection, man will have to totally rely on his senses, instincts, and his ability of reason. Man's instincts will be formed by what he perceives to be true and by what information is stored in his subconscious mind.

Once you are born again, the Holy Spirit delivers information to your spirit man. Dr. Paul Yonggi Cho says in his book, *The Fourth Dimension*, "What is the subconscious? The subconscious is your spirit. The Bible calls the subconscious the inner man, the man hidden in your heart." Once spiritually alive, we are not to merely rely on the information gathered by our natural senses. The subconscious mind is where spiritual insight and intuitive thought is received.

The subconscious is like a database or a computer hard drive—it stores everything it hears and/or sees. It has the ability to collect information at an incredible rate. When you walk into a room for the first time, the moment your feet hit the floor of that room your subconscious has already collected and filed into its database just about every article of clothing that each person is wearing. However, our conscious mind will not recall all the information that is stored. There are ways to develop your memory recall so that you will be able to draw a greater amount of this information.

When I was young, I abused my mind and body with a lot of drugs, so much so that I lost much of my memory. Later, when I was born again, I asked God to heal my memory and increase my memory recall. Within a short period of time, my memory and my ability to recall from my subconscious was restored. Some people call it a photographic memory. Through developing your imagination, you will learn to rely on pictures and pictures are the way of communication and the way that we pull from our subconscious.

PREJUDICE VOIDS CREATIVITY

Most Christians become nervous when they hear the word *psychic*. *Psychic* simply means to have a supernatural or clairvoyant ability. God has given all of us this type of supernatural ability. We don't have to be prophets to hear from God; every believer has the ability to hear from his Father. A prophet has the responsibility of speaking to God's people regarding His intentions in the earth, whereas each and every one of us has the right to receive direction, encouragement, and inspiration from God. According to the new covenant, we all can hear and receive from the voice of God. I believe that Moses' prayer was answered by God when He said, "Are you zealous for my sake? Oh, that all the Lord's people were prophets and that the Lord would put His Spirit upon them!" (Num. 11:29) God has placed His spirit on all flesh, and we all can prophesy. There is a difference between someone who can prophesy or hear the voice of God and someone who is called to speak to the Body of Christ on behalf of Christ.

I use the word *psychic* so that I can broaden your understanding. We instantly identify that word with sorcery and soothsaying, and rightly so, because the most common use of the word is used in the world and New Age circles. I think as Christians, we should avoid all appearance of evil, but we should have a clear understanding of what we are avoiding for the sake of witnessing and communicating to the unsaved. For example, many of us would say that we don't believe in psychic abilities. Is that true according to the real definition of *psychic*? Of course not. We do believe in receiving insight and supernatural clarity, but we don't believe in the source where "psychics" get their information—from evil sprits—whereas Christians receive their insight from the Holy Spirit.

Ignorance is the foundation of prejudice. Some of the most prejudiced people in the world call themselves Christians. Certain Christians become so dogmatic they don't research other cultures, choosing to remain ignorant. We see it every day. People prejudge other people because they have a different skin color, income bracket, and even denomination. We can't seem to work together simply because someone wants to worship Jesus on Sundays while someone else chooses Saturdays, or because they play drums in their church, or speak in tongues, or baptize in a different way. Ignorance is the best friend of prejudice, and prejudice is the best friend of segregation. I am not saying that we shouldn't hold on to our doctrines; I am saying that we should seek unity and express God-likeness in the earth.

Jesus prayed in John 17:11, "Now I am no longer in the world, but these are in the world, and I come to You. Holy Father, keep through Your name those whom You have given Me, that they may be one as We are." We need to seek unity, and while we are seeking unity, we will find our common ground. I don't want to do anything that will bring the wrong understanding to Christianity or Christ. Yet on the other hand, we should seek to understand and then seek to be understood.

Generalizations can be strongholds that have been formulated through a religious spirit, prejudices, or the traditions of man. I have watched people miss the greatest opportunities because of a religious spirit. For example, we will never win the world by talking our Christianized subculture language. So often, Jesus said things in His day that offended the religious hearers, because He wanted to confront some wrong and limiting thinking. Christians are the worst at creating mental limitation when they hear or read something that challenges their generalizations and prejudices.

The words *clairvoyant* and *psychic* are associated with the New Age movement, so we stray away from using such words simply because we would rather be ignorant rather than expand our understanding through communication and study. The Webster Dictionary defines *clairvoyant* as "having or claiming to have the power of seeing objects or actions beyond the range of natural vision." As a Pentecostal or charismatic preacher, I fully embrace seeing beyond the natural—I want the supernatural. Of course, we don't want to be identified with anything that is unrighteous; but on the other hand, we must not formulate opinions based on limited understanding. We must be willing to research and learn, allowing God to show us how He wants to lead us and teach us. I want to see and receive from the supernatural. We can no longer be one step behind the world.

The Pharaoh of Egypt had sorcerers with serpents and supernatural abilities, yet God didn't shy away from sending His own seer to perform supernatural deeds. Moses was sent to Pharaoh's court with abilities that were even greater than Pharaoh's sorcerers.

There was a notable difference between Pharaoh's sorcerers and God's prophets. While Pharaoh's sorcerers were immorally inspired and used their ability to manipulate others, God's intention was and is to inspire mankind to its greatest end—to help us to become fruitful, multiply, subdue, and take dominion.

CONSCIOUS VERSUS SUBCONSCIOUS

We receive spiritual messages through our spirit man, but are not able to communicate these messages until we receive them consciously. Our spirit man possesses the senses of spiritual sight, hearing, smelling, tasting, and touching; and the Holy Spirit communicates to us through these five spiritual senses. The conscious mind must receive these messages from the subconscious in order to produce fruit. This is where most people cut off the supernatural thought. Once you begin to dream a dream, or see a vision, your conscious mind will automatically research reasons why this creative thought should be impossible.

121

That's where the war begins. Your subconscious desires the un-seen possibilities, and your conscious or your rational mind weighs the odds. Reason takes its toll and you dismiss the cre-ative thought as an emotional imagination. In your conscious mind, prejudices and religious ideologies reside and they con-front creative thoughts, intuition, and prophetic revelation the moment your conscious mind receives the divine revelation from God. Hence, it is very important that you overcome strong-holds and prejudices.

From experience I know that the only way to overcome strongholds and prejudices is by using your seeing ability as often as possible and by receiving an image and dreaming of yourself living and walking in that image. You must see before-hand what you believe God has called you to live and walk in. You must see your destination before you can achieve your des-tiny. Most millionaires who I know are driven by a divine sense that they are destined and gifted to achieve financial excel-lence. They sow with clarity, living the lifestyle long before they achieve it. If you believe that God has called you to be a million-aire and can see yourself as a millionaire, then you must picture yourself living in the mansion, shopping at the appropriate stores, driving the car of your dreams, and becoming so wealthy that you can give away 90 percent of your income and still live comfortably on ten percent. These things are possible if you believe.

The Scripture is clear in Matthew 17:20: "So Jesus said to them, 'Because of your unbelief; for assuredly, I say to you, if you have faith as a mustard seed, you will say to this mountain, "Move from here to there," and it will move; and nothing will be impossible for you.' " Faith, even faith as a mustard seed, is the ability to see it before you have it. What does a seed do? It repro-duces. If we have faith that can produce what we see, then it can make that which seems unlikely and even impossible, possible, even to the point of moving mountains. How unlikely does that seem? Yet, if we have the faith of a mustard seed, we will produce the impossible.

Faith is first seeing. You must take and save snapshots of your future in your present conscious state of mind. The outcome of your future depends on your ability to see it before you receive it. What you see, you will automatically move towards. There are times when I am driving in my car that I turn my head to the left to look over my shoulder so that I can change lanes. My hands begin to move in that direction even before I decide to make the complete change.

When I was just a boy, I learned how to catch a football. My uncle told me to keep my eyes on the ball and my hands would follow. Once the ball was thrown, my eyes followed the ball until it reached my hands. When it fell into my hands, I grasped the ball just as I had imagined it. At first, catching the ball was a little awkward, but after additional practice and by using my new ability to catch, I was able to catch fast passes, long passes, high passes, and even kicked footballs. My ability increased the more I used it. Again, I want to quote something from Dr. Paul Yonggi Cho in his book, *The Fourth Dimension*. He says, "My ministry has been revolutionized by discovering the truth of the fourth dimension, and you can revolutionize your life with it. You may wonder how we can incubate our subconscious. We dwell in limited bodies, whereas the Holy Spirit in His omnipresence can simply incubate over the whole earth. But we are so limited in space and time, and the only way for us to incubate is through our imaginations, through our visions and our dreams."[4]

IMAGINATION

Science says that if you don't use your mind, you will lose it. The brain cells that you do not use will die without being replaced. Therefore, we must maintain a constant mind-set of growing and learning. Many people stop learning once they are out of school. The world is in a state of switching our imagination off until we are in a crisis that forces us to find a way out. Most people believe that only children need an imagination, when in actuality, we will never be able to see beyond obstacles without using our imagination. By using our imagination, we can envision ourselves out of the crisis and troubles that we may be currently experiencing, creating new thoughts of joy based on an imaginary future.

Simply because a thought has entered into your mind through the imagination does not mean that it is fantasy. Leanne Payne says in her book, *The Healing Presence*, "For many Christians, raised on the King James Bible, the word (imagination) may hold distinctly negative connotations, for it was used in that translation to denote a scheming or devising mind. This may be one of the factors behind the irrational fear of the imagination, which we find in some Christian circles. The imaginative faculty, like any other human faculty, can be used for good or evil. To ignore or fear it is dangerous, and is a kind of evil, just as misusing it is evil."[5]

She also writes in her book some information from her own research of the meaning of *imagination*: "The dictionary defines imagination as 'action...of forming a mental image or concept of what is not present to the senses.' Another definition denotes the imaginative faculty itself by which these images or concepts are formed. A third meaning refers to the 'power which the mind has of forming concepts beyond those derived from external objects (the "productive imagination").' This power refers not only to fancy but to creative or poetic genius, 'the power of framing new and striking intellectual conceptions' (Oxford English Dictionary)."[6]

If you, as an adult, examine a child's play, you may think it is foolishness. Yet, Jesus said that we must become like a child in order to experience the Kingdom of God. As adults, we tend to take life extremely serious and because of the seriousness of our view on life, we turn off our imagination in order to grasp reality. Unfortunately, the more realistic you behave, the less imaginary you become, resulting in a lack of creativity. People who maintain a creative imagination will oftentimes be labeled eccentric, because others decide that those people cannot differentiate the real from the imaginary. Yet, most successful inventors have been considered eccentric; nevertheless, many inventors have found the balance between real life and fiction by focusing their imagination on problems instead of using it for daily living. Most adults don't exercise their imagination; hence, they lose it. The less you use it, the harder it will be to reactivate.

Thomas Edison journalized his problems each evening before he went to bed, which allowed him to sleep on his problems. Even though your conscious mind sleeps, your subconscious mind never does. That part of your mind deciphers and interacts with your imagination even while you sleep. This is why you will often have a solution to a problem the moment you awake. Many times I tell people to spend time listening for the creative thought in the morning because your spirit man or your subconscious mind has been listening to God during the night and will try to relay that information to your conscious mind. Your imagination allows you to create new mental habits, which will automatically work themselves into your daily behavior.

Dr. Maxwell Maltz writes in his book, *Psycho-Cybernetics*, "Science has now confirmed what philosophers, mystics, and other intuitive people have long declared that each human being has been literally 'engineered for success' by his Creator. Every human being has access to a power greater than himself."[7] I have said for years that science is man trying to explain the greatness of God. We are made in God's image—how can we be created for anything other than success! If you will take a moment to think about that every day, I believe this truth will change your life. The Bible says that we have been fearfully and wonderfully made.

To many people, this section will sound mystical and superstitious, yet we must understand that the human being has been created for success and God has placed what scientists now call "cognitive mechanisms" in our soul. Science says this is the ability to convince yourself of a fact that will form your emotions, stimulate your nervous system, and even create success in people conditioned to failure. Your mind is not a machine, yet it can be developed and expanded just like a machine through constant and repetitive information, resulting in mental habits and desires. Your emotions and nervous system can be fooled by what you believe. Napoleon said, "Imagination rules the world."

Snapshots of Success

Creative thoughts—snapshots of the future—will increase the more you desire them. This is why we must exercise possibility thinking and possess a positive mind-set. Nothing is impossible in the eyes and heart of God. If you can receive a snapshot, you can also receive what you see. God can do exceedingly abundantly above all that we ask or even think. He will never allow us to see something that is impossible.

When I was in elementary school, we made cameras. We put photo paper into a box that had a hole in the front of it that was covered with masking tape. Once I pulled the tape back to expose the photo paper to the light, the light activated the photo paper. The light imprinted an image onto the photo paper causing it to reproduce what was seen. Your subconscious mind is like the photo paper. When you receive a creative thought, that thought becomes an image of your future illuminated by the possibility of God's goodness and imprints the image of your future into your mind.

Creative thoughts are snapshots of the future and answers to present problems. They are images of success and images of solutions. And just as every other pioneer and inventor has done, you must *desire, receive,* and *act* upon these snapshots as well. Snapshots cannot come to pass without these three ingredients. You must become emotionally involved with the dream. Until your emotions are allowed to run their course, you will see these snapshots as ideas only and not as your destiny. Emotional conviction will produce the momentum necessary to follow out the dream and overcome the voice of reason.

Creative thoughts must become more than what you hope to do, more than what you are called to do, more than what you dream to accomplish. They must become who you are in regard to your destiny and your victory over your need.

ENDNOTES

1. Paul Yonggi Cho, *The Fourth Dimension,* 17.

2. Theodore Levitt, *The Marketing Plan* (New York, NY: The Free Press, 1983), 127.

3. "Pictures, Photos, and Quotes of George Washington Carver." *Inventors.* About, Inc. Copyright: 2005. Date accessed: May 2002. http://inventors.about.com/library/weekly/aa041897photos.htm.

4. Paul Yonggi Cho, *The Fourth Dimension,* 43-44.

5. Leanne Payne, *The Healing Presence,* 163.

6. Ibid.

7. Maxwell Maltz, *Psycho-Cybernetics* (New York, NY: Pocket Books, 1960), 27.

CHAPTER SEVEN

FEAR FACTOR

Fear not, for I am with you; be not dismayed, for I am your God. I will strengthen you, yes, I will help you, I will uphold you with My righteous right hand (Isaiah 41:10).

Fear is a most wretched emotion. It destroys your confidence, minimizes your dreams, and isolates your productivity. Fear is the enemy of success, the nemesis of hope, and the opposite of faith. Yet even though fear is a most powerful opponent, it cannot exist where there is a strong conviction toward a dream, and it is overcome when you see beyond the possibility of failure. When success is imminent, the power of fear will lose its controlling and manipulating force.

THE SPIRIT OF FEAR

There was a time in my life when I was so controlled by fear that I had an extremely difficult time leaving my own house. I would go to great lengths to avoid any public place. There were times that I would leave my house to attend church, but I would return as soon as possible to avoid any kind of interaction.

It started one day when I awoke from a bad dream. I had just returned home from ministering on the street and laid down for a quick nap. In the dream I was preaching and praying for the sick on the street when suddenly I heard a voice say to me, "If you don't stop, I will kill you!" The voice was so clear it awakened me. I instantly sat up and realized it was a dream. So I laid down again and fell back to sleep. Once asleep, I had another dream—I was walking down the street and a car was coming deliberately toward me to run over me. As the car approached me, I heard the voice of fear again, saying, "If you don't stop, I will kill you!" Startled, I woke up again. I was very frightened. Even though it was just a dream, I was afraid.

The voice of fear is very convincing. I did what most of us do when we first feel the grip of fear—I rehearsed the possibilities of what the voice of fear spoke to me. Over and over in my head I heard the voice until I was convinced that it was true. At that point, whether it was possible or not, my mind made it true. Fear feeds off the insecurity of an unsure future. It shows a false reality. I was miserable for months. My life basically stopped, my ministry halted, my dreams were shattered. Anxiety mastered my life. I hid it behind smiles and charismatic statements, but I was dying daily. It had gone on too long for me to stop. I needed help.

As I watched television one day, I heard an evangelist, James Robison, tell a story about one of his family members being bound by fear, so much so that he was hearing voices. (During my times of ministry, I have seen the spirit of fear cause schizophrenia multiple times.) After telling the story, he prayed for those who were watching the broadcast to be free from fear. Immediately, I felt free. Of course, I had to change the way that I was dealing with fear. I couldn't be passive toward negative thoughts; I had to be aggressive and confront the negativity before it overwhelmed me.

Jesus never allowed negative thoughts, negative words, or negative people to be around Him without His confronting the negativity with the positive. Sometimes we think that if we ignore negative things, they will just leave. But to pretend something is not there is the worst thing you can do. Negativity doesn't disappear by ignoring it; instead it grows into a nightmare. When satan approached Jesus with negative words, Jesus replied with contradictory words—words of hope.

I could have avoided all this misery if I had immediately confronted the negative thoughts with the truth. When you remove negativity, you take away the foundation of fear. Instead of rehearsing the negative, I should have rehearsed the possibility of the help of a good God and the promise of a good life. Fear will always try to capture you, yet you can stay free by replacing each fearful thought with thoughts of hope every time it raises its ugly head.

The Bible says, "God has not given us a spirit of fear, but of power and of love and of a sound mind" (2 Tim. 1:7). Remember that fear destroys your confidence, minimizes your dreams, and isolates your productivity. But God has not intended for us to live in fear. Instead, He has made provision so that we can be free from fear.

POWER

First, realize that you are not powerless. God created us in His own image and ability. Man has power to overcome anything that is hindering him. Inside of us we have the authority to stomp hatred and viciousness into the ground, and we have power over any other enemy of our future. Nothing can injure us. Luke 10:19 says, "Behold, I give you the authority to trample on serpents and scorpions, and over all the power of the enemy, and nothing shall by any means hurt you." The Greek word for "power" used in this Scripture is *exousia* (ex-oo-see´-ah), meaning "delegated influence and authority." Authority gives you the ability to walk. Authority speaks of action. It allows you to walk in the fullness of your jurisdiction. The spirit of fear desires for you to become paralyzed even though you have the power to walk anywhere and do anything that your jurisdiction allows. God has given you power to walk over anything that would undermine your authority within your jurisdiction. Your jurisdiction is based on what your calling is or based on what creative thought you have received from God. Creative thoughts give you a surveillance of the jurisdiction that God has delivered to you.

If you never start walking, however, you will never possess the possibilities. All things are possible only if you step toward the possibilities. Don't wait any longer; don't allow fear to restrict you to a life of mediocrity. Move forward! Move on with God into your destiny. Just take a step in faith, and you will experience what you have been dreaming.

LOVE

"Perfect love casts out fear" (1 Jn. 4:18). Fear involves torment, whereas love involves confidence. God is love, and in love is the ability to accept, believe in, and cherish an imperfect person. Knowing that God accepts you, no matter what you have done and where you have been, allows you to walk in your jurisdiction with confidence. The Bible says that love has been made complete because Jesus has positioned you, just as He is positioned.

> *Love has been perfected among us in this: that we may have boldness in the day of judgment; because as He is, so are we in this world. There is no fear in love; but perfect love casts out fear, because fear involves torment. But he who fears has not been made perfect in love* (1 Jn. 4:17-18).

Jesus paid a great price for us to experience the benefits of Heaven here on earth. The favor and love that Jesus experienced from the Father is the same favor that those who believe in Him can receive. When Jesus taught His disciples how to pray, a part of the prayer was to ask for the benefits and authority of the Kingdom of Heaven to come into our lives here on earth. God loves us so much He wants to give us the benefits of Heaven, here on earth.

When we receive Jesus as Lord in our lives, we become the children of God, just as Jesus is the Son of God. As adopted children, we are heirs of eternal blessings in Heaven as well as recipients of eternal blessings in this present world. Our inheritance includes strength, prosperity, protection, health, success, and guidance. Love never leaves you lonely and alone; love fights for those whom it loves; love sacrifices for the benefit of the loved one. Dr. Maxwell in his book, *Psycho-Cybernetics*, says, "God does not see us as pathetic victims of life, but masters of the art of living; not wanting sympathy, but imparting help to others, and therefore thinking less and less of our ourselves, and full, not of self-concern, but of love and laughter and a desire to serve...."[1]

Our confidence comes from the understanding that our heavenly Father has a watchful eye on us, making sure that our needs are met. John, one of the 12 apostles wrote about himself as "the one whom Jesus loved" (see Jn. 19:26). I have often thought, *How could he have so much confidence of Christ's love?* It wasn't until I had my own children that I finally realized where his confidence came from.

For example, there are times as I am watching television that one of my sons will sit on my lap and lay his head on my chest. As a father I can't help but to kiss his head and whisper in his ear, "I love you." As I read the Bible, I notice that John positioned himself in a place to hear his Savior say, "I love you." "Now there was leaning on Jesus bosom one of His disciples, whom Jesus loved" (Jn. 13:23).

My children do not doubt that I love them because they hear it and see it all the time. This gives them confidence in who they are. Love removes all desire for approval, love removes insecurity, and love removes all self-esteem issues. An intimate relationship with God causes us to understand true unconditional love. Unconditional love builds confidence within us toward God's attitude and intentions toward us, confidence that He wants only the best for us. Jesus is at the right hand of the Father enjoying the presence of God and the benefits of Heaven. God wants to also give us on earth the benefits of Heaven that Jesus is experiencing now. This is love's confidence.

A SOUND MIND

Let's talk about mind over matter. Your thoughts control your actions. To have soundness of mind is to have mental self-control. When people see or hear of someone who has engaged in an act of violence, destruction, or nonsocial behavior, I often hear them say, "What was he thinking?" But herein lies the problem—he probably *wasn't* thinking. It is amazing how often folks don't take time to think through their actions and reactions. People's reactions to fearful circumstances are usually not the wisest ones. It begins with your thoughts. If you can't control your thoughts, you will never control your destiny. Mental focus is the key to success. Remember that faith causes sight that will produce, but you must learn to maintain that sight through the storms and the obstacles that come.

Discipline is the same as self-control. Without mental discipline, you will be unable to conquer the fear of failure, the fear of man, or the fear of commitment. Without discipline, you will not be able to balance the opportunities that will come because of a creative thought and emotional reactions.

Mentally disciplined people are thinkers. Unfortunately, most people choose not to use the most important tool available to them—their mind. Fear stops you from thinking, fear stops you from dreaming, fear stops you from learning. The brain is a muscle, and it grows stronger with mental exercise. Remember, when we don't use our mind, we lose our mind. The brain cells that you don't use will die. In order to stay mentally strong you must keep your brain in a constant state of learning. The Greek word for "sound mind" literally means, "saving the mind." We protect our mind by pulling on the reins of our mind, by challenging ourselves to think deeply and learn new things.

There is an old saying, "An idle mind is the devil's playground." A mind without voluntary thought will have its space taken up with immoral and unproductive ideals. King Solomon, one of the wealthiest and wisest men who ever lived wrote, "Whoever has no rule over his own spirits is like a city broken down, without walls" (Prov. 25:28). A city without walls is vulnerable to its enemies. Thoughts that destroy all possibility of success will enter your mind when there are no guards or belief systems developed beforehand. Sin will enter in and corrupt all creative thoughts. Sin's best friends are condemnation, guilt, and shame. These four enemies of success will consume your dream bit by bit and piece by piece until you have procrastinated the time and desire away.

Procrastination is a lack of self-discipline and the by-product of fear. Many people have lost the greatest opportunities of their lives by waiting just one more day. (But if you can put it off until tomorrow, you can do it today.) Some opportunities may be lost even within an hour. Remember—just get it done, because if you wait until tomorrow, you will have to do today's duties as well as tomorrow's. Set daily standards of self-discipline.

In order to achieve success, you must develop systems in every area of your life. Adam and Eve were given a chance to create their own system, but they wreaked chaos. After that, God worked on a plan to get man back on track by placing mankind in a system. Franchises work because they are predesigned systems that are fail proof as long as you follow the system. Success comes from either developing a system or following and adhering to a system.

God said to Noah when he and his family left the ark, "While the earth remains, seedtime and harvest, cold and heat, winter and summer, and day and night shall not cease" (Gen. 8:22). Mankind would never have the same opportunity that Adam and Eve had; the system had been set. You reap what you sow! If you sow laziness, you reap laziness. If you sow in time management, you will reap additional time and more opportunities. Success habits beget success. Gain control of your life, and in the future, you will thank God that you did. There are discipline tools available to help you set your life in order. If you can prioritize your life activities, responsibilities, and your time, you will maximize each opportunity that comes in the future, simply because you have developed a system of discipline that can handle future success. I have always heard that if you want something done, you should delegate it to a person who is already busy because he already knows how to get things done.

King Solomon also said, "[God] stores up sound wisdom for the upright; He is a shield to those who walk uprightly" (Prov. 2:7). God will deliver to us wisdom and protection if we walk uprightly. Walking uprightly is dependent upon how you control your thoughts. An upright person protects his mind because he understands that the battle is in the mind. If you are weak in your mind, you will be weak in other areas of your life as well. If you lack discipline, you will be undisciplined when it is absolutely critical that you exert self-control. You must learn to celebrate discipline; otherwise, you will never learn to become a disciple.

It is most important to be willing to develop a sound mind and take consistent steps toward saving your mind. In order to change a negative habit, you must contradict that habit daily with a new habit for a certain period of time. Some experts say it takes 21 days to form a new habit and to break an old one. You will need to meditate on creative thoughts for at least 21 days in the morning and before you go to bed, in order to really begin to take ownership of the dream. Meditation is the most powerful tool for positioning yourself for your future. In the next chapter, we will give you a deeper understanding of the lost skill of meditation.

ENDNOTE

1. Maxwell Maltz, *Psycho-Cybernetics* (New York, NY: Pocket Books, 1960), 44.

— CHAPTER EIGHT —

MEDITATION

Do not let this Book of the Law depart from your mouth; meditate on it day and night, so that you may be careful to do everything written in it. Then you will be prosperous and successful (Joshua 1:8 NIV).

There are many forms of meditation. In this study I will pinpoint the two that I am familiar with. My reference for these is based upon researching the Bible, which I conducted for my personal benefit. I felt I was missing something in my devotional time and knew that meditation was necessary for further personal development. I also felt that modern religion was neglecting a powerful, commanded form of communication with God, by neglecting to meditate. The Bible has been written as the inspired Word of God; in addition, it is full of cultural practices, practices that are not familiar to Westerners. Meditation is one of these practices. We will refer to the passage of Scripture where apostle Paul instructs the church of Philippi, and we will also look at the instance where he instructs Timothy regarding meditation. Meditation is a wonderful yet underestimated form of prayer. The Nelson's Illustrated Bible Dictionary, in a commentary on meditation says, "Meditation is a lost art for many Christians, but the practice needs to be cultivated again."[1]

My goal is to help you understand that meditation is actually first designed and ordained by God and is not only a mystical and occult form of worship. The forms of meditation we will discuss will not bring you into an altered state of mind, although they will change the way you think and dream. At no time will you lose your ability to make conscious decisions, which dangerous forms of meditation will do.

INFINITE INTELLIGENCE

Meditating on the proper ideas and in a proper way will lead you to success and prosperity. It is without a doubt that if you read the following pages carefully and follow their instructions, you will increase your effectiveness and influence within a short period of time. You will begin to attract to yourself successful association and become aware of previously unseen opportunities. Proper meditation taps you into God's creative abilities allowing Him to overrule your inability, transforming you into your full potential.

Napoleon Hill wrote in his book, *You Can Work Your Own Miracles,* "I began to make inquires of the hundreds of successful men who collaborated with me in the organization of the 'Science of Success,' and discovered that each of them had received guidance from unknown sources."[2] Hill continued by listing such men as Thomas A. Edison, Henry Ford, Luther Burbank, Andrew Carnegie, Elmer R. Gates, and Dr. Alexander Graham Bell. Each and every one of them described to Mr. Hill his personal experiences. Dr. Bell, in particular, believed that he was aided by a direct contact with, in his own words, "Infinite Intelligence."

The modern mind-set, which says that God is only for the ignorant man or someone like a drug addict who needs a lift, was not the belief of the genius pioneers of technology. God is still the "Infinite Intelligence" that He was when the earth was created, when the lightbulb entered into the mind of Thomas Edison, and when the Model T became a dream of Ford's. The greatest mind is the mind that we have available to us; the Bible calls it the "mind of Christ" (see 1 Cor. 2:16). If we can see what God sees, then we can accomplish what He is showing us. Your destiny is set and your future is bright, but you must overcome any ghost of the past that affects your present. The way you see life now will directly affect the way you view tomorrow.

ATTITUDE OF GRATITUDE

Let's look at the first form of meditation, which we find in Philippians 4:8-9:

> *Finally, brethren, whatever things are true, whatever things are noble, whatever things are just, whatever things are pure, whatever things are lovely, whatever things are of good report, if there is any virtue and if there is anything praiseworthy—* **meditate** *on these things. The things which you learned and received and heard and saw in me, these do, and the God of peace will be with you* (emphasis added).

The writer of this passage instructed the Philippians to meditate on positive things—think on things that have positive virtue to them. We all know that it is naturally easier to dwell on the negative rather than the positive. However, we must be aggressive toward keeping a positive outlook. Steer away from negativity and complaining—they attract only trouble, and I am persuaded that they hinder any angelic assistance God wants to provide.

I remember years ago when I was feeling sorry for myself, I heard a still small voice say to me, "Go to the convalescent home on Sunday after church." If you have ever visited a convalescent home, you already know that it is nearly impossible to stay ungrateful for what you have when you see and talk to people who, all of a sudden, woke up one day and couldn't move, walk, or take care of themselves, people who lost all their independence and former quality of life. When I walked out of the convalescent home, it was as if someone had removed dark glasses from my eyes. I had the same experience when I went to visit the children living in the dumps of Tijuana, Mexico, and also when I visited Tanzania, Africa, to minister to the Rwandan refugees. I saw the place where millions were murdered and the devastation that was left behind. Sometimes it is best to put yourself into humbling situations and give yourself a culture shock so that the universal law of humiliation can squash all pride in order to prepare you again for success.

If you are in a season of pity, I suggest that you take the time to visit someone who is in a worse position than yourself. This will help you to consider your blessings and appreciate what's in your hands now.

Taking Inventory

The New Testament of the Bible was written in Greek and the Greek word for "meditate" is *logizomai* (log-id´-zom-ahee), meaning "to take an inventory." When things seem to be looking grim and there is no end in sight, you should not look to the future, but you should remind yourself of the pleasurable and enjoyable times of your past and the blessings of the present. The Torah uses the Hebrew word "musing," when Isaac went out to meditate on the day that he met his wife, Rebekah. Isaac went to a private place to reflect as in the sense of praying. This is a time of reflecting on the goodness of God. Remind yourself and proclaim to God that your life is not your own and that the battle is not yours, but His. This is the time to take inventory of all the blessings you have in life—time to remember how God has delivered your family from worse situations.

There is something miraculous about gratitude. Once you become grateful for what you have, supernatural things seem to fall into place and hope appears in the same manner the sun rises in the morning. Many times, we are far better off than we realize. This knowledge comes when we find the time to take inventory of what we already have. Unfortunately, we often don't take the time to consider what we have, until we've lost something we have taken for granted or until we get into trouble. Troublesome times can force us to take a hard look at what we have been given. Being grateful for what is in your hands now is the key to getting more into your hands in the future. Let me explain with a story from Second Kings 4:1-7.

The bill collectors were harassing a widow after her husband died and left her without provision for herself and her family. As described in the Bible, she relayed her problem to the prophet Elisha and the prophet asked her, "What do you have in your house?" She replied, "Nothing but a jar of oil." Suddenly, the prophet heard the voice of God saying to him, "Tell her to borrow as many jugs as she possibly can and then take and sell the oil I will supply." This was the creative thought. Immediately she obeyed the thought and borrowed as many jugs as she thought she would need.

The supply of oil continued until all the jugs were filled; then she sold every jug she had. When it was all said and done, she had enough money left over after paying her bills to take care of her family. God didn't give her a handout; He gave Elisha and her a creative thought that produced more success and fulfilled more than just her need. Handouts are good for the poor, but "hand–ups" are even better. The widow would have never thought about that jar of oil if the bill collectors had not called. She took inventory because she desperately needed a way out. Your need will cause you to take inventory, and God will give you a creative thought that will lead you into the greatest success you have ever experienced.

A man named Strauss used what was already in his hands, and God gave him the creative thought to meet the need of some gold-digging miners and of generations to come. When the California gold rush was in full swing in 1850, everyday items were in short supply. Levi Strauss, a 20-year-old Bavarian immigrant, leaving New York for San Francisco, carried with him a small supply of dry goods. Once in San Francisco, a prospector wanted to know what Mr. Strauss was selling. When Strauss told him he had rough canvas to use for tents and wagon covers, the prospector said, "You should have brought pants!" and proceeded to explain that he couldn't find a pair of pants strong enough to last through the tough terrain and work.

So Strauss made pants from the canvas. The miners liked the pants, but complained that they tended to chafe. Levi Strauss, up to the challenge, substituted a twilled cotton cloth from France called "serge de Nimes," which became known as denim.

In 1873, Levi Strauss & Company began using the pocket stitch design, and the two-horse brand design was later used in 1886. The red tab attached to the left rear pocket was created in 1936 as a means of identifying Levi's jeans at a distance. All three are registered trademarks that are still in use today.

Decide today that your current needs may be the key to your big break. You may have been looking for your big break in all the wrong places. A great opportunity often comes after your worst moment, when the imagination works the hardest to solve the problem.

REVOLVING THOUGHTS

The second form of mediation is found in First Timothy 4:14-15:

> Do not neglect the gift that is in you, which was given to you by prophecy with the laying on of the hands of the eldership. **Meditate** on these things; give yourself entirely to them, that your progress may be evident to all (emphasis added).

The Greek word for "meditation" used in this passage is *meletao* (mel-et-ah´-o), meaning to "revolve in the mind, to imagine, (pre-) meditate, to practice."

Revolving a meaningful thought over and over in your mind, engraves the image into your subconscious, causing an action to follow. The image that you revolve in your mind will eventually become the pattern for your life. If you revolve failure in your mind, you will fail; if you practice defeat in your mind, you will be defeated. The children of Israel thought and claimed themselves to be grasshoppers in the sight of their enemy—without ever consulting their enemy. The children of Israel superimposed the image they had of themselves and assumed that that was how their enemy perceived them as well. Your perspective of yourself is the key to your future.

When I was in high school, I skipped my speech class when I was scheduled to speak in front of my classmates because I couldn't see myself as a public speaker. Standing in front of a group of individuals was my greatest fear. Later, when I felt a call to preach, I started to imagine myself preaching in front of thousands with confidence. When the time finally came for me to stand in front of a crowd, there was no more fear. It was gone and only confidence remained. Practicing meditation is the only way to brand a creative thought into your subconscious mind. Once this image is a part of your imagination, your life will conform to what is in your soul. The Bible commands us to renew our mind. The only way to do that is to revolve the promises of God, the creative thoughts, the solution to your need, in your mind until it becomes one with you, resulting in the inevitable manifestation.

A scientific experiment was conducted with three groups of students. The experiment had to do with increasing skill in shooting free throws during the game of basketball. The first group shot free throws every day for 20 days, and each student was tested on the first day and the last day. The second group didn't practice at all, and they too were scored on the first and last days. The third and final group spent 20 minutes a day, imagining that they were shooting free throws. If they missed the free throw in their imagination, they would simply adjust it in their mind, allowing them to correct their skills as they re-volved it in their minds. They were also tested on the first and last days.

The results were remarkable. The first group who physical-ly practiced every day for 20 days improved by 24 percent. The second group, who did not practice at all, showed no improve-ment. The final group, who practiced only in their mind, im-proved by 23 percent!

A preliminary study was conducted at the Cleveland Clinic with 30 healthy volunteers using sophisticated brain imaging technologies to study the power of the mind, true mind over matter. The first group practiced mental contractions of the muscles in their hand; a second group practiced mental con-tractions of muscles in the elbow, and a third group, practiced neither. Again the results were phenomenal. Strength in the hand increased by 35 percent, while the elbow and the bicep in-creased by 13 percent. The results of "muscular thinking" lasted for three months after the volunteers discontinued the mental training.

The reason for giving you the information above is to help you understand the power of mental meditation. It will help you see yourself free from anything that holds you back. I believe that if you suffer from the control of a negative habit or an uncontrol-lable addiction, 99 percent of your deliverance is you doing some-thing or your "acts of faith," and one percent is God's help and His miracle-working power. If a person cannot control his ap-petite, he must begin to imagine himself free from the bondage and living in the freedom that is available to him. Whether it's eat-ing disorders, fear, pornography, or fits of rage, these emotional-ly induced sins can be overcome simply by renewing your mind daily, through revolving images that contradict your present failure. But without your ability to see yourself free, freedom will never last.

THE MENTAL ADVANTAGE

Mohammad Ali used to posture himself as the victor before he ever entered the boxing rink. He spoke what he imagined so fervently and consistently that when it came time to do it, his body took hold of it and performed what he had imagined. He could already see the new champion's belt in his home; he could already see the headlines of the next day's newspapers. He never allowed defeat to defer his dream; he simply adjusted mentally what needed to be adjusted and continued to refer to himself as "The Champ." This is posturing! You must posture yourself mentally now, so that you will be transformed into what you desire in your future; and when something tries to contradict your dream, you must mentally readjust yourself to the pattern of your future.

In the book, *Think and Grow Rich,* author Napoleon Hill tells a story of an inventor by the name of Elmer R. Gates. Dr. Gates created more than 200 useful patents, through the process of cultivating and using creative thought. Mr. Hill states that Dr. Gates had a private room in his laboratory, which he called his "personal communication room." In this soundproof and light tight room, he had a table with a notepad on it and a push-button panel across from him where he could control the lighting. The following words are Mr. Hill's own words to describe the genius, Dr. Gates:

> When Dr. Gates desired to draw upon the forces available to him through his creative imagination, he would go into this room, seat himself at the table, shut off the lights, and concentrate upon the known factors of the invention on which he was working, remaining in that position until ideas began to "flash" into his

mind in connection with the unknown factors of the invention.

On one occasion, ideas came through so fast that he was forced to write for almost three hours. When the thoughts stopped flowing, and he examined his notes, he found they contained a minute description of principles, which had not a parallel among the known data of the scientific world. Moreover, the answer to his problem was intelligently presented in those notes.[3]

I must let you know that Dr. Gates was paid greatly by some of the largest corporations in America during his era for "sitting for ideas." Mr. Hill wrote something after his statements about Dr. Gates that I think are very important.

The reasoning faculty is often faulty, because it is usually guided by one's accumulated experience. Not all knowledge that is accumulated through experience is accurate. Ideas received through the creative faculty are much more reliable, for the reason that they come from sources more reliable than any which are available to the reasoning faculty of the mind.[4]

This technique of the communication room should be used by all of us when confronted with a decision, a problem, a crisis, an invention, and even a new ministry or business idea. Genius inventors have learned to retrieve information from the invisible realm to apply to our daily life. These inventors would dream of a product, think on it intently, seeing every angle, and every detail. Then they would pursue the end product. If for any reason they found a glitch or something didn't work the way they expected, they simply returned to the detailed mental drawing to see what could be wrong. After long and hard gazing at the invisible, their attention would be directed almost automatically to something that they had never noticed before. When we receive the thought, the thought is complete in the sense that God has delivered the full ability to accomplish what you see.

Remember, God will never allow you to dream of something that is impossible. With His help, all things are possible. When you pursue something you have been dreaming of and you run into a glitch, simply return to the drawing board in your mind. Revolve the end result in your mind. See yourself accomplishing what you have been hoping for. See yourself living your dream. Do this every day, and you will accomplish it. Miracles still happen and God is still a miracle worker. The reason many have not received the miracles they have hoped for is because we have not been taught how to receive a miracle. It's simply seeing and living it long before you have it.

Instead of seeing meditation as some form of mysticism, we must understand that the biblical form of meditation is mental focus. Mentally focus on the goodness of a great God; mentally focus on the possibility of health and prosperity. Mental focus is a vital part of your future.

In Maxwell Maltz' book, *Psycho-Cybernetics*, Dr. Harry Emerson Fosdick is quoted as saying, "Hold a picture of yourself long and steadily enough in your mind's eye and you will be drawn towards it. Picture yourself vividly as defeated and that alone will make victory impossible. Picture yourself vividly as winning and that alone will contribute immeasurable success. Great living starts with a picture, held in your imagination, of what you would like to do or be."[5]

Meditation builds new thoughts and strips negative and disappointing memories from their power, convincing you of the possibilities of all that you dream and hope for. Faith is the confidence that what you have focused on mentally was destined to be yours from the foundations of the world and that it will make its way to you in due time. Once you begin to focus mentally with the confidence of receiving prosperity, God will begin to work with you to accomplish it.

ENDNOTES

1. *Nelson's Illustrated Bible Dictionary* (Nashville, TN: Thomas Nelson Publishing, 1986).

2. Napoleon Hill, *You Can Work Your Own Miracles* (New York, NY: Fawcett Columbine, 1971), 46.

3. Napoleon Hill, *Think and Grow Rich* (Fawcett Crest, NY: Napoleon Hill Foundation, 1960), 181.

4. Ibid., 182.

5. Maxwell Maltz, *Psycho-Cybernetics*, 45.

— CHAPTER NINE —

KEYS TO THE KINGDOM

The entrance of Your words gives light; it gives understand-ing to the simple (Psalm 119:130).

My eyes are awake through the night watches, that I may med-itate on Your word. (Psalm 119:148).

I once read a story of a great warrior, Hernando Cortez, who assembled men and equipment during the 1500s and set sail for Mexico from Cuba, landing on what is now the state of Tabasco. During the battle with Indians there, he took many captives, including a young Aztec princess who became his inter-preter and advisor. Cortez continued up the coast, and on April 21, 1519, he landed near the site of Veracruz. There, to prevent all thought of retreat, he burned his ships. This action gave his men no option but to succeed.

At one time, during a battle with a warlike tribe of natives, Cortez and his men were outnumbered 300 to 1. However, they were victorious, and eventually, on November 8, 1519, Cortez reached Tenochtitlan (now Mexico City). Although he established a relationship with the Aztec emperor, Montezuma, many Aztec warriors continued to attack Cortez.

At another time, Cortez and his army defeated 1,400 soldiers that Diego Velasquez, the governor in Santiago, had sent to bring him back to Cuba. Most of the survivors joined Cortez. He and his army continually battled Aztec warriors against great odds, and in 1521, he and his soldiers eventually destroyed the great empire of the Aztecs.[1]

When you choose to attempt the impossible, you will need to destroy all possible opportunities of retreat, just as Cortez destroyed his ships. The Scripture we studied in the last chapter on meditation—"Meditate on these things; give yourself entirely to them, that your progress may be evident to all" (1 Tim. 4:15)— is written with the same mind-set. Once you have a clear and definite creative thought to meditate on, you must burn any bridges of retreat and failure.

The Leap of Faith

I remember when I was a young boy, a group of friends and I went to a river to jump off the bridge into the water below. I watched as one after another of my friends climbed over the rail and plunged off the bridge. I myself had never jumped off a bridge before, and the closer it came to my turn to jump, the faster my heart began to beat. Though I could swim, I wasn't a confident swimmer, and thoughts of the worst possible things began to race through my head. First, I imagined I hit my head and drowned in the water. Then I imagined I hit the bottom of the river, broke my legs, and was unable to swim to shore. Then I imagined I made it through the jump without hitting my head, but I saw myself unable to reach the shore because I was such a weak swimmer. Meanwhile, my friends kept egging me on to jump, so I slowly climbed over the rail. I looked at the 80-plus foot drop, closed my eyes, and leaped. Seemingly, time stood still. In mid-air I opened my eyes and said to myself, *Why in the world did I do this?* Everything in me wanted to return to the bridge; I wanted to be safe again. But of course, I had absolutely no control. By the time I finished that thought, I was already swimming to the shore. Once to the shore, I couldn't wait to get back to the top to try it again.

"Giving yourself to it" and "jumping off the bridge" are synonymous. If you will take a risk and jump off the bridge, giving yourself completely to the dream, you will ultimately experience victory. If you experience victory once, you will understand that you can experience victory again.

Your victory is to be evident to all. Everyone should see your prosperity. Many will look at your life and desire to change because of what they have seen happen to you. I believe that there will be a noticeable transformation in your life through the ability to cultivate and receive creative thoughts.

Jesus understood that nothing was impossible to man if he could tap into God's possibilities. He also understood that it was not what entered into the mouth of man, but what was in the heart and thoughts, and what came out of the mouth of man that destroyed his possibility. So when Jesus said to His disciples that they must ask, seek, and knock, He was giving them the keys to receive and cultivate creative thoughts. He handed them the keys to the Kingdom.

ASK

To ask, you must first realize you need help. Once you understand that you need help, you must put yourself in a position to be helped. Jesus said that if you ask, it "shall" be given to you. So the real key is asking. When you have a problem, ask; when you have a goal, ask; or when you have a dream, ask.

Creative thoughts come to minds that are looking for answers. If you are not open to hear, then you will never hear. The quest for knowledge is the beginning of gaining knowledge. Because Dr. Gates had a room, where he was secluded and undisturbed, he was in a position to receive. He made specific provision for himself to receive. When you position yourself to receive, you have asked loud and clear. If you don't have the time to separate to a quiet place, then you don't have the unadulterated desire for a creative thought. Remember, what you receive as a creative thought can change your life forever.

One 30-minute session in the communication room can solve a problem or give you an invention. You can't afford not to take the time. This should be done for 15 to 30 minutes—once in the morning and once in the evening. There are times when I will wake in the middle of the night with ideas flowing through my mind. If this begins to happen to you, then keep a notepad by your bed and write down any thoughts that interrupt your sleep. Some will be very good and some will be hardly worth the lost sleep. In any case, waking up in the middle of the night is but a little price to pay in order to find a brilliant answer to a stubborn problem. Sometimes you may feel inspired in the middle of the day. The object is to remain flexible and willing to receive. It will also depend on the urgency of your need. In crisis, I find myself meditating at odd times of the day, especially if my thoughts start to become negative. Other times, I am wide open to receive anything I can receive.

Don't be disturbed if the first time, or even during the first 30 times, you receive nothing. Nor should you be weary of waiting if you can't receive an answer when you most need it. It takes time and practice to recognize what you are looking for. Sleep on it. Your subconscious mind and the Spirit of God will continue to work on it as you sleep. Nothing is achieved by struggle, so relax and be confident that there is One who is more interested in you than you can ever imagine.

Seek

Once you receive creative thought, you must not neglect it or brush it off; you must continue to concentrate and focus on the picture. The more you look upon it, the clearer it will become. If you will be faithful with little, then more will come to you. Remember, your ability to see clearly and hear clearly develops and increases merely by using it. " 'Consider carefully what you hear,' [Jesus] continued. 'With the measure you use, it will be measured to you—and even more. Whoever has will be given more; whoever does not have, even what he has will be taken from him' " (Mt. 25:29 NIV). The Amplified Version actually reads a little clearer, "The measure of thought and study you give to the truth you hear will be measure of virtue and knowledge that comes back to you—and more besides will be given to you who hears." How much you put into applying the creative thought is how much you will get out of the creative thought. If you seek to understand and seek to walk it out, then you will receive more thoughts and more understanding. If you stop prematurely, you may be cutting off millions of dollars or missing an answer to a possible lifelong situation. If you seek, you shall find.

Seeking should involve speaking. During your 30-minute communication session, you should verbally describe the creative thought out loud, as you receive it and as you revolve it in your mind. Describe it in as much detail as you possibly can. Do this daily. It may feel a little awkward at first, but you will soon notice the difference in your confidence level and your actions toward the desired goal. If you are imagining yourself free from annoying habits, please remember to revolve in your mind the freedom of not being reliant and dependent on these things. You will not overcome these habits on your own; the Holy Spirit will work with you as you meditate and dream. As you reformat your mind, the Holy Spirit will help you become who you are destined to be. Imagine yourself never desiring to raid the refrigerator again in the middle of the night. Imagine yourself turning down the fattening and sugar-loaded chocolate cake at the birthday party. Then imagine your health and energy returning to you as you had when you were a little girl or boy. See yourself not ever having to give food another thought and instead directing your energy into lasting and important things. You can dream yourself out of an eating disorder or a sugar addiction if you truly desire to be free.

I have talked to many men who have been bound by sexual addictions. Sexual addiction is the enemy's attack on the imagination of males. Men have been induced with testosterone for the purpose of conquering and taking dominion, and they are designed to use this testosterone in conjunction with positive imagination to see themselves being successful in business, ministry, or any other calling of God. But the enemy has tempted men to be distracted by vain and perverted imaginations, causing them to squander their creative imagination on uncommon and perverted pleasures. This is a waste of the God-given success drive that God has given men for victory. These men find themselves so bound by their imagination that even if they are married to lovely, wonderful women, it soon destroys their marriage because the imagination is more pleasurable than real love and communion.

In your mind anything is possible, but when a situation doesn't play out the way you planned it, it causes your heart to grow frustrated and sick. I hear men say it all the time—"We just grew out of love." Yes you did…because your imagination wasn't kept pure and undefiled but developed an improper focus. High sex drive is not only for the intimacy of a man and a woman; it is given for man to exert energy and excitement in conquering. If you're a slave to sexual habits, dream yourself free; imagine you do not enjoy impure imagination. See yourself disgusted with it in your mind and see yourself helping other men free themselves from the problem. Give your mind to this for 21 days in order to develop a mental habit, and watch what happens to your actions. It's not easy, but it's very necessary.

The Holy Spirit will be your helper and comforter. You can't overcome without help, yet you cannot receive the help of the Holy Spirit without a mental transformation. The Holy Spirit cannot help you if you continue to think the same way. That's why you must meditate on those things that are pure. You cannot change your pattern without reestablishing a new pattern. Your wife and children will notice a difference, your friends and coworkers will notice a difference, and you will notice a difference. Do not waste your God-given ambition on unproductive imaginations that will never become reality and that are simply destructive and negative. You know that a thought is destructive if it encourages you to break covenant. Your imaginations should never cross the lines of covenant. Keep the covenants with your wife, family, friends, and God in your mind, and you will keep those covenants in your life.

See yourself free and speak yourself free.

I learned a great lesson from my mother who taught me something that changed my life, yet she never realized she was part of such valuable instruction. It happened when I was nine or ten years old. Before I tell you this story you must understand that my mother was a 15-year-old girl when she gave birth to me. She did the very best she could in raising me. I don't blame her for anything, nor do I regret my life or upbringing. I am who I am because of her.

When I was young, my mother sometimes called me "stupid" if I did something wrong. After a while I started referring to myself as stupid. I would say it all the time. If I made a mistake, any mistake, I would yell, "Man, I am so stupid!" Soon my academic abilities started to reflect my words. I went from an A student to an F student within months. First my grades declined, then my attitude, and lastly my character. I spent my later years in school believing I was stupid. It wasn't until I left high school and started studying business that I realized I wasn't stupid at all. And it wasn't until I became a Christian that I realized that God didn't make me stupid. But even though I realized I could learn and I had a capable brain, I still had no confidence in my abilities or a desire to learn because I had brainwashed myself into stupidity.

I can remember the day that I received a creative thought telling me that I had talked myself into stupidity and I had learned to be stupid by repetitively speaking what I thought to be truth. Then I thought that if I could talk myself into stupidity, I could also talk my way out of stupidity through repetitively speaking what I could believe for. So, daily I would verbally confess, "I can learn" or "I am a genius" or "I have a photographic memory." Soon I began to love studying; I became energized by learning new things. You must begin to talk to yourself, not foolishly, but purposefully. The more you speak it, the clearer you will see it.

After you see it clearly and speak it, then you must pursue it. Start working on it even though you may not feel ready. Start moving toward it. Doors will open to those people who are trying to find them.

Knock

Knock and it shall be opened to you. This basically means don't give up even though it looks like you have hit a dead end.

One night while driving home late, after spending time with some friends, I noticed that the traffic lights changed from red to green immediately before I got to them, if I drove the speed limit. So I tested this theory. I increased my speed until I was exceeding the speed limit between the traffic lights, and I found myself waiting at each and every red light. Then once again, I decreased my speed to the speed limit, and again, the lights changed right before I approached them. The lesson is: Doors don't open when you want them to open. Doors open when you're in the right place at the right time for the right reason.

Knocking is about going back to stage one if you have to. Sometimes a closed door plainly means you need to refocus— go back to asking and seeking to make sure that the vision is clear. It also could mean you need to be patient because you're being developed to eventually handle the dream. Either way, the door will always open, if you keep knocking. Closed doors are usually a timing problem.

"Ask and it will be given to you" is used twice in the Bible. In Matthew chapter 7, it is used in the context of not giving valuable things to an individual who has no respect for what you're giving them. "Do not cast your pearls before swine" (see Mt. 7:6). What's more, in the same context Jesus said, "What man would ever give his son a rock when he asked for bread?" (see Mt. 7:9) "None, in their right mind," I say when I read these words. Furthermore, Jesus continues by saying, "How much more will your Father who is in heaven give good things to those who ask Him?" (see Mt. 7:11)

The second use of this phrase is used after Jesus tells a story of a man who went to his friend because he was in need of some bread (see Lk. 11:9). The friend refused to answer the door and give bread to his friend because it was late at night. However, through persistence the man would get as many loaves as he needed (see Lk. 11:8).

The bottom line to knocking is first having an enormous desire to receive, a desire fueled by a need or a dream. Secondly, realize that you will not be pursuing this desire on your own but you will have the help of your Father in Heaven. Finally, persist beyond the "No's", beyond the failures, beyond the disappointments. Persistence can give you what even your best friend won't. If at any point in the process you feel like giving up, it is because you have stopped meditating and have become too busy with merely seeking. Meditation keeps you peaceful, confident, and calm through the difficult seasons.

CULTIVATING CREATIVE THOUGHTS

1. Daily set apart a time and place for meditation. Make this place special—a place where you cannot be disturbed. If you

have children, you may have to wake up a few minutes earlier or stay up a few minutes later. Make your goal 30 minutes, but you will do well starting off with 10 to 20 minutes.

2. Take a notepad and pen with you. You won't always have new thoughts; nevertheless, you want to be ready if creativity begins to flow. Many times you will simply spend time meditating on the thoughts you have already received. Remember, the goal is to meditate on creative thoughts that will invent a new you, a new product, a new direction, a new family life, even a different way of living. Dream and imagine the future, seeing all the limitations that have been placed on you removed. See yourself just as you hope to be. See the invention prototyped, marketed, and in the hands of the consumer. See your new company in full force and making profits, or if you're an entertainer, see yourself on stage or on the big screen with millions watching. It's your dream, so dream big. If at any time, you see in your mind's eye the direction changing course, write it down and log it for later reference. We see only in puzzled pictures or as through smoky glass, so some of the information may come later as you continue to ponder on your dream and cultivate the creative thought. Remember, first you see it, and then you verbally describe it. Do this in private so that you can speak it without being concerned of what people think. Never feel obligated to share your creative thoughts; people will eventually see it come to pass.

3. Make sure that you also write down what you're willing to lay down and sacrifice for this success. Success always comes with a price. Jesus paid the price, yet we cannot possess what God intends for us to have if we keep doing the same things that previously caused failure to reign in our lives.

4. Make sure that you write down the creative thought in great detail. Fix your mind exactly on what you desire. Make it a definite purpose for your life. Write exactly what you see as the

end result of your dream. Then meditate and recite the dream daily.

5. Take action whenever actions are available to you, and start immediately. Create the best plan possible with the information and ability that is available to you now. Procrastination is one of man's greatest sins. If you wait to be ready, you'll never be ready. You won't be ready before you move. A parked car is hard to steer. So just move! If you follow steps 1-3 daily then all that you need will come together automatically as you move. Your movement will generate an irresistible attraction of people, events, and opportunities that will help you see your creative thoughts come to pass.

ENDNOTE

1. Anthony Pena. "The Untold Story." *Christopher Columbus and Astrology*. About, Inc. Copyright date: 2005. Date accessed: May 2002. http://library.thinkquest.org/J002678F/cortez.htm.

— CHAPTER TEN —

TIMING

He has made everything beautiful in its time. Also He has put eternity in their hearts, except that no one can find out the work that God does from beginning to end (Ecclesiastes 3:11).

The most frustrating thing in my life is waiting for something I have been hoping for or something I have been diligently working towards. Every person who has felt a sense of destiny and has been working hard to achieve a dream has experienced this same frustration. God has given man stewardship over everything on the earth except for time. No matter how hard we try, we can never manipulate time.

When I was a child, my favorite movie was "The Time Machine." Even today, I can't resist seeing the modern version of "The Time Machine." I have often wished I could go back in time to change my past. There have been many times that I wished I could reverse that thing that caused me to be put on restriction as a child. What is man's fascination with time? It is the only thing beyond man's control.

The one certainty about time is that everything under the sun has a moment of completion, an appointment of maturity, a mandate of fruition, a time of purposeful beauty, an end. Solomon said that everything is beautiful in time.

YOUR APPOINTED TIME

So many people with gifts or talents get overlooked because their time of revealing has not yet come. Our development is like the development of a rose. No one has a full appreciation for a rose that has been picked before its maturity. A green little rosebud is not very valuable until it has begun to grow and blossom. The beautiful petals have not yet revealed themselves through the green leaves, nor has the lovely fragrance begun to permeate the body of the bud. At this point, there still needs to be more growth, more development. If it is plucked too early, the maturing will stop and the true value will never be revealed. The rose should have ample amount of time to mature while still connected to its roots. The roots allow nutrients to flow to the bud as long as the stem and bud are still connected, and in due time the day of beautification will present itself. Someone will then pass by who appreciates the beauty of the rose and will pluck and set it on his or her table. The lesson to learn here is to stay plugged into whatever source of growth and development you have available to you, whether it be church, school, a personal mentor, or some other authority.

In Acts chapter 3, there was a man who had been lame since birth. For years, he was daily stationed at a gate called Beautiful so that he could beg for a living. The Greek word used for the name of the gate "Beautiful" means "belonging to the right hour or season (timely) or the appointed time." Then finally one day, some of Jesus' disciples, Peter and John, saw him, and as they approached the man, they commanded him to look at them. Once they had his attention, they performed a miracle through the power of God.

I believe that even though this man didn't have any idea in his mind that he would be healed through this miracle, he did have enough expectation to receive his healing—not because he was looking for a miracle but because he was in the right place at the right time, expecting something good. The best way to overcome the frustrations of time is to first realize that God has given everything a time of beauty and to simply wait in the proper posture to receive it once the timing and your prepared-ness meet. I once heard a millionaire say that if you desire to be a millionaire, you must do something every day to achieve that destiny. Our posture or positioning is everything. If we stop pos-turing ourselves and move out of position before the proper timing, it could be devastating to our destiny.

The Bible speaks of an appointed time in Habakkuk: "Then the Lord answered me and said: 'Write the vision and make it plain on tablets, that he may run who reads it. For the vision is yet for an appointed time; but at the end it will speak, and it will not lie. Though it tarries, wait for it; because it will surely come, it will not tarry' " (Hab. 2:2-3). The instruction is very clear. Plainly write the vision so that people who read it will follow the same path they see you successfully pursuing.

Even here, the Bible says that the dream is for an appoint-ed time, reserved for a fixed time. The next portion of this Scripture may sound contradictory, yet with further research it reveals a wonderful and refreshing insight: "Though it tarries, wait for it; because it will surely come, it will not tarry." In its original text, the Hebrew language reads, "Though it seems questionable or hesitates, adhere yourself to it as if you were glued to it, because it will surely come to pass, it will not loiter nor will it procrastinate, but it will manifest at its perfect time." The purpose of God is never late; it is always at its perfect time. When God places a vision in your heart, He also calculates the timing of its fulfillment. We tie ourselves to the creative thought until it comes to fruition, and waiting is the only way to make sure that you are ready for the appointed time. We must adhere ourselves to the vision; otherwise, if the vision lingers, we may find ourselves distracted and settling for less than God's perfect will.

Waiting for Your Opportunity

We must understand that sometimes our victory is delayed because God is setting the circumstances in order, circumstances that will set us into the right place, at the right time, for the right reason. Joseph's undesirable circumstances were far from accidental. God will move the hearts of kings, stop the sun, and even cause a famine just to get us into the right position. We can get a quick glimpse of this in Psalm 105:16-19: "Moreover He called for a famine in the land; he destroyed all the provision of bread. He sent a man before them—Joseph—who was sold as a slave. They hurt his feet with fetters, he was laid in irons. Until the time that his word came to pass, the word of the Lord tested him."

God called a famine in order to position Joseph in the right place, in order to fulfill His promise. Yet as God was working on Joseph's destiny, God had to also work on Joseph. Let's read it again: "They hurt his feet with fetters, he was laid in irons. Until the time that his word came to pass, the word of the Lord tested him." Joseph went through abnormal pain during this season of preparation. Most people seek to take the easy route during the most important times of preparation, but there is a restricted period of time that this can take place in. Notice the words, "Until the time." Remember, God will not allow you to be tested beyond your ability to stand; the trial will end before you break, if you tie yourself to the vision. If you don't break under pressure, then your creative thought will come to pass, just as you have dreamed it.

The word of the Lord tested Joseph, and the word of the Lord will test you and me. What does that mean? Again we must go to the original text, which reads, "The word of the Lord fused to him as metal fuses together under intense heat." As you are adhering yourself to the creative thought, God is stoking the fire in order to adhere the creative thought to you. As we said in an earlier chapter, the vision must become more than a creative thought; it must become part of you, your destiny. This happens only when you have passed the test of time, the test of fire, and the test of defeat. If you're still willing to fight for it, then God will join with you in the fight, even changing circumstances in order to position you for the fulfillment of the creative thought.

MANKIND AND TIME

Why did God create time? God created time because of purpose, because without purpose there is no need for time. Timing gives a certainty that what we are trusting to happen will come to pass. Time exists for us, we do not exist for the sake of time. We cannot control time because we cannot control our purpose. A man's purpose is given and designed by God; therefore, God and God alone can control the timing and purpose of man.

Time creates two emotions within us. The first is ambition or drive to accomplish what we feel is so urgent that we may not have enough time to accomplish. The second is a fight for patience. Time makes you feel anxious in both of these ways, anxious to accomplish your goal and the anxiety of the goal being delayed.

Christopher Columbus felt the race against time. In *History, Prophecy, and the Stars*, Laura Ackerman Smoller writes about Christopher Columbus, "Astrology dictated that the world would endure only some 155 years to come. Preceding its destruction, however, Columbus told the monarchs: all of the races would be converted to Christianity. He saw his own voyages as part of the universal missionizing of the last days."[1]

Christopher Columbus believed that he was a part of the last-day missionaries who would turn the world around. This urgency caused him to risk his life and his reputation in order to accomplish his goal. Neither the fear of death nor the fear of failure could persuade him to abandon the trip. His sense of timing also caused him to be persistent enough to return to the queen of Spain regardless of her negative reception to his first inquiry. Time caused him to feel the urgency of the hour and the urgency created persistence and patience.

Joan of Arc received her first revelation at the age of thirteen and a half. Even though she had doubts at first of hearing her mission, by the time she reached sixteen and a half she received a direct command from God to help the soon-to-be king by approaching Robert Baudricourt, the commander of Charles VII. One month later, she stood before Baudricourt, yet he treated her with no respect, saying, "Take her home to her father and give her a good whipping." This was the first of many rejections she would endure. Nevertheless, Joan didn't back down from her call. Even though she often would reply to God regarding her call, "I am a poor girl; I do not know how to ride or fight." The voices simply replied to her, "It is God who commands it." This ardent response from God moved her to action. Her destiny was affirmed; the mission moved on. She returned to see Baudricourt. Some accounts say that on this visit, he drew his sword to attack her. As he did so, she grabbed a dagger and blocked the sword. Suddenly, Baudricourt's sword broke in pieces. Needless to say, he believed in her mission from that point on.

As the situation for King Charles grew worse and the voices grew more urgent, Joan disguised herself as a man for protection and journeyed to Chinon. Charles VII tested her by disguising himself, but she at once saluted him without hesitation amidst a group of attendants. Charles VII was quickly impressed with her revelation, for she gave him a private sign that only he and God would know of. After all of these accounts, she still pressed on. The day of appointment had to come because it was her purpose to see it fulfilled.

Next, numerous committees examined her before she could be involved with the military. These committees were designed to test her for soundness. The bishops and doctors who governed the meeting were impressed with this poor peasant girl. After this proving, Joan returned to Chinon to lead the troops to victory. The king offered her a sword, but she refused. Instead she sent word to have a search conducted under the alters in the chapel of Ste-Catherine-de-Fierbois to look for an ancient sword buried there. It was found in the exact spot that God told her it would be found. With destiny, there is always supernatural provision.

In the first battle, Joan suffered an injury, which she prophesied would happen. Even though she was wounded, she insisted that the campaign continue. This was because the voices told her that she *had only a year to accomplish her mission,* and of course we know that her mission was a success. I tell you these accounts because I want you to understand that patience will have its perfect work. Once patience is finished, urgency will prod you on until you finish your mission.

TIME WILL TELL

Time builds patience when you are being developed, and time destroys procrastination once you are filled with urgency. Whether it's consistency and persistent prodding or whether it's the quick pace of urgency, each one is the work of the enigma of timing. One thing we do know about time is that it always runs out.

Thomas Edison said, "Genius is one percent inspiration, 99 percent perspiration." He also said, "In trying to perfect a thing,

I sometimes run up against a granite wall a hundred feet high. If, after trying and trying again, I can't get over it, I turn to something else. Then someday, it may be months or it may be years later, something is discovered... which I recognize may help me scale at least part of the wall..."[2] The creative thought never left him no matter how long it took him to accomplish the goal. This is true persistence, and persistence is drawn out of you once you have battled the nemesis of timing.

You may be mastering persistence, as Thomas Edison had to master it before he finally figured out the incandescent lighting system. No one could figure out how to make the lightbulb practical enough to use in homes and other buildings. No one could create a bulb that could be used in another place other than for outside lighting, such as a street lamp. Bulbs for street lamps were too bright and luminous for indoor use. Edison eventually created a bulb and a lighting system that made lighting your home and other closed areas possible. It was practical, safe, and economical. It is said that this took some time and something like 1000 attempts. One thousand attempts at anything will definitely make you a master of persistence!

In order to master persistence, you must become a slave to time and a servant of purpose. I believe that he learned this from his mother. It is said that Thomas Edison was a poor student and that his teacher called him an "addled." His furious mother took Thomas Edison out of school and home-schooled him herself. Edison later said, "My mother was the making of me. She was so true, so sure of me, and I felt I had someone to live for, someone I must not disappoint." The patience of Edison's mother, to teach a boy whom his teacher called mentally confused or as rotten as an egg, had to have taken extra time—time, which nurtured the genius out of a misunderstood boy. This time had to have created persistence in him, a patience and persistence that has truly changed the world. This is how God deals with us—He teaches us patience because He understands that if we are persistent and patient, then timing will work the good for us.

Nothing is impossible with God's help, if you give it some time.

ENDNOTES

1. Laura Ackerman Smoller, *History, Prophecy, and the Stars* (New Jersey: Princeton University Press, 1994), see also http://astrology.about.com/od/celebrityfamous/l/aa050102a. htm.

2. Gerald Beals. *Thomas Edison Quotes.* Copyright date: 1996. Date accessed: May 2002. http://www.thomasedison.com/edquote.htm.

MINISTRY CONTACT INFORMATION

Tracey Armstrong
P.O. Box 78096
Seattle, WA 98178
Telephone: 206-722-5757
Church: The Citadel www.thecitadelseattle.com
Ministry: Lionheart Minstries www.lionheartministries.com

Additional copies of this book and other
book titles from DESTINY IMAGE are
available at your local bookstore.

For a complete list of our titles,
visit us at www.destinyimage.com
Send a request for a catalog to:

Destiny Image® Publishers, Inc.
P.O. Box 310
Shippensburg, PA 17257-0310

*"Speaking to the Purposes of God for This
Generation and for the Generations to Come"*